Peace in our time?

PEACE IN OUR TIME?
Some biblical groundwork

David Atkinson

GRAND RAPIDS, MICHIGAN
WILLIAM B. EERDMANS PUBLISHING COMPANY

For Jonathan and Rachel

Library of Congress Cataloging-in-Publication Data

Atkinson, David John, 1943-
  Peace in our time?

  Bibliography: p. 221
  1. Peace — Biblical teaching.
  2. Peace — Religious aspects — Christianity.   I. Title.
BS680.P4A85   1986   241'.6242   85-27458

ISBN 0-8028-0179-X

Contents

Preface

If I were asked – as quite properly I should be – to justify adding one more book to the already over-weighted piles of literature on this subject, my reply would be twofold. First, this is written primarily with Christian students in mind, and although I do not think that I say much that hasn't already been said – and often said better – elsewhere, I do think that I am bringing together into one book diverse material which may not all be readily available to the average student.

Second, and more important, I am concerned that too much of the current Christian literature does not root its moral judgments adequately in theology. No doubt some will feel that mine fails at this point also, and many others will disagree with the theological stance which I adopt. But I believe that the primary task for Christians engaged in discussion of moral issues is to think theologically. So I have had a go.

My working title for this book was *The Ways of Justice and of Peace*, which I still like, although it was too cumbersome to go on the cover. It captures the double thrust of the task to be undertaken in this area: to explore Christian ways of establishing justice as well as Christian ways of making peace – and, indeed, illustrates how the two belong together in this fallen world, 'until justice and peace embrace'.[1]

This book simply documents how far I have got. There is a long way to go, and I do not pretend to offer anything more than work in progress. But I hope that it points a direction sufficiently clearly to help others on their way.

I owe a debt of gratitude to several people who have criticized parts of this book at various stages, but I must single out Mr Graeme McLean for special thanks. He has argued with me at length, and saved me from some of the more obvious blunders. I am sure he will think that too many still remain, but he knows my immense gratitude for his help.

David Atkinson

---

[1]To borrow the title of a book by N. P. Wolterstorff.

Part 1

James is confused

James is very confused.

He has just seen the television news reporting that a group of women has been arrested at Greenham Common in Berkshire; they are to be charged with causing a 'breach of the peace'. The women had climbed the perimeter fence of the US Air Force base, and danced on the site that was being prepared for part of the batch of 160 Cruise missiles which in 1979 NATO had decided should be based on British soil. In fact the NATO decision was to deploy a total of 572 American nuclear missiles in Europe: 108 Pershing II missiles, with a range of about 1,000 miles, based in the Federal Republic of Germany; and 464 Cruise missiles based in Britain, Italy and, it was hoped, Belgium and Holland. The Cruise missiles for Britain were allocated to Greenham Common in Berkshire and Molesworth in Cambridgeshire, though at a time of nuclear alert they would be driven from these bases and dispersed around the countryside up to a hundred miles from their bases.

It was against this decision that the women were protesting. They had been doing so for a long time. And James has every sympathy with them. If these missiles were ever fired, they could well contribute to a 'breach of the peace' in Europe on a scale never before witnessed on this earth.

James respects these women. As a Christian student he has been deeply influenced by the teaching of Jesus: 'Love your enemies'; 'Do not resist one who is evil'. He simply cannot square these Christian convictions with the build-up of nuclear stock-piles. James has read E. P. Thompson's essay 'Protest and Survive', and agrees that to plan for a nuclear war is a form of madness. He sees the force of the Campaign for European Nuclear Disarmament. He was struck by the newspaper headline: 'If there are enough nuclear weapons now in Europe to destroy the continent 30 times over, what does it matter if one side can do it 14 times and the other 16?'[1]

James has also read Jim Garrison's book *From Hiroshima to Harrisburg*[2], with its devastating and appalling accounts of the physical, psychological and social effects of the bombs dropped on Hiroshima and Nagasaki in 1945. He knows that the Russian SS20 missiles, against which the Cruise missiles are described as part of a 'balance', each have a destructive power of several hundred times that dropped on Nagasaki. He has read of the suffering, the devastation, the radiation danger, the inability of such medical services as might survive to cope, the psychological and physical disorders which last for decades. Such a bomb must *never* be allowed to be used. We must get rid of such weapons. Surely the women at Greenham Common are right to protest.

But then James reads other literature which suggests that disarmament is a dangerous delusion. The road to real insecurity in the West would be to take any steps now which would alter the balance of nuclear power. The idea of a nuclear-free zone is a utopian picture, out of touch with either the realities of the long, hard, laborious process of negotiation between governments, or the real threat posed to the security of the West by the anti-Christian ideologies of Euro-Marxism and the immense nuclear capabilities of the Soviet Union. Christians are among those who are urging the maintenance of a strong nuclear deterrent. While love for enemies may be capable of expression between individuals, in the 'real world' of international politics, can such naïve idealism have any place? The real way to secure a reduction in the likelihood of war is to match strength with strength, and so enable the government to negotiate from a strong bargaining position. Alongside this, when James reads some of the literature about Christian believers suffering for their faith in Communist lands, he feels the force of the appeal to stand against the 'Soviet threat' in the name of justice and freedom. After all, the prophet Amos in the Old Testament made much of social justice, and Paul in the New Testament seems to indicate that part of the purpose of the state is to maintain order. James reads of Christians who, while committed to arms reduction, nevertheless are convinced of the need for a strong nuclear capability as a bargaining counter in negotiations, and a strong nuclear deterrent as the most likely means of maintaining peace and order. James sees the weight of the argument that justice sometimes needs enforcing.

So he is confused.

James is confused also because as a citizen he wishes to exercise his vote responsibly. How should a Christian citizen view his political responsibilities? Is he called 'out of the world' to be a visible demonstration of an alternative to the materialistic, economics-dominated society around him? Or should he play his full part in seeking to bring his society into line with Christian values?

Then there was that awful weekend when he had been away with friends. His host was driving him back to the station when the traffic was stopped for the parade to go by: the band, the colours, the soldiers, the medals, those carrying wreaths. It was Remembrance Sunday. Over the war memorial was a large white banner inscribed in heavy black letters two feet high: 'We shall Remember'. His host turned to James with pain in his voice. 'Some of us', he said, 'are trying to forget.' He had been called up in 1940 to fight for King and Country. He had gone with a willing enthusiasm in 'the cause of freedom'. He had served well, was a good soldier.

9

But he had killed a German. That had haunted him in his dreams every night since. The German had had a family, dependants, loved ones; and he had killed him. In the course of duty. It had been one or the other. Yet he was now in bondage to the nightmare of what he had done. Oh yes, he had acted rightly. In his mind he could marshal all the arguments together. He had acted on orders in the cause of liberty. But now he was trapped in the prison of his remorse: he had killed another man.

What would James have done in his position? That German soldier was precious in God's sight. Could James have done that terrible thing? Perhaps he would have been a conscientious objector? But does that have much meaning in the context of possible wars in which the distinctions between combatants and non-combatants seem in practice increasingly blurred? If there were ever to be a nuclear exchange, the idea of 'non-combatant immunity' might mean very little. Perhaps everyone was now involved whether they liked it or not? And words which might have had meaning once: 'chivalry', 'valour', 'courage', would lose their meaning in the unspeakable squalor and devastation of modern technological warfare.

So James had mixed feelings on Remembrance Sunday. He recalled with gratitude those who had given their lives for the freedom he now enjoyed. But he felt also the pain of his host who wanted to forget. And he felt a deep unease. The parade, the thanksgiving, the remembrance of 'our glorious dead', somehow seemed to make war itself glorious. And that troubled James's Christian conscience very much.

James is also rather afraid. He hopes that before long he will get married, but he fears for the sort of world into which he will bring his children. Fellow students seem to talk quite openly about their belief that they will not see out their natural life, so certain do they seem that a nuclear holocaust will overtake them. So let them eat and drink and be merry, for tomorrow they die. Such fatalism cannot be right, thinks James as a Christian. But how is he to square the threat of the mushroom cloud with his deep faith in the providence of a gracious God? If this really is God's world, what does that imply for the way James thinks about the future? 'Be of good cheer, I have overcome the world' seems to ring rather thin as Cruise and Pershing missiles are being made operational.

James's own future is also insecure. He is nearing the end of an engineering degree, and has recently been for interview with a major British electronics firm. Would he be willing to 'tackle defence work', he had been asked. He said he hadn't really thought about it. He didn't get the job. He wasn't sure that he had wanted it. But so much of the national budget was going on 'defence', and so much scientific work in the major industrial companies was related in one way or another to 'defence' that it was difficult to see how he could get a job without contributing in some small way to the arms race. Would he be willing to work for 'defence'? What did his Christian faith mean for him in a decision like this?

James is confused. He is trying as a Christian to get his thoughts in order. He wants to bring his confusion under the rule of Christ. He wonders what the Bible says about war, and whether this will touch the decisions of today's world. He would be interested to know how other Christians have handled some of these questions in the past.

I have written this book in an attempt to help him. It does not talk about military strategy: that is a task for military strategists. It does not venture very far into political decisions. It does not presume to tell James what he should think, or how he should vote, or which jobs to apply for: that is for him to decide. It does, however, try to sketch out some Christian theological themes which should have relevance for the Christian soldier, the Christian politician and the Christian citizen as they make up their minds. It does not pretend to be more than a sketch, but I have listed a few books at the end, if James wants to pursue the matter.

While my own views inevitably show through, my main aim is to give some theological groundwork on which arguments

11

can be based and decisions made. I hope that those who disagree with my own conclusions will nevertheless feel that I have been fair to their viewpoint.

Let me explain the order of the chapters. Part 2 is background to our primary task. Firstly we look at what the Bible says about war and some related themes (though James may be rather disappointed that the Bible does not seem to touch many of today's questions at all directly). Then we sketch out various traditional Christian approaches. Again we will need to be very aware that modern warfare poses altogether new questions which some of the great theologians of the past could not have glimpsed. Finally in this section we look briefly at some contemporary political history.

All this is the setting for our primary task which begins in Part 3 – that of setting out a theological foundation on which to build our own responses to biblical and traditional viewpoints, and to our contemporary situation. This theological foundation is the heart of the argument, and to my mind the most important section in the book. Part 4 moves from theology to ethics, and to my own conclusions and questions about war and deterrence. Finally we try to take stock, to say where we have reached and indicate what still remains unsure.

It is my hope that this will be of some use to James. If it encourages him, or anyone else, to take up the military or political implications in more detail, that is all to the good. If it pushes him to write to his MP or take other action with a view to bringing our national priorities and national decisions more into line with the faith that this world belongs to a God whose nature is holy love, so much the better.

May God direct this nation and every nation in the ways of justice and of peace; that men may honour one another, and seek the common good.

Notes for Part 1

[1] *The Guardian*, 30 November 1981.
[2] SCM, 1980.

Part 2

Clearing the ground

Introduction

We begin with some perspectives from the past, and with a look at some of the biblical material. Some has been interpreted in favour of Christian pacifism, some in a way which allows for the necessity for war in a fallen world.

Until recently it was possible to divide the traditions of Christian attitudes to war broadly into these two strands. The majority strand, which includes great teachers of the church such as Augustine, Aquinas, Luther and Calvin, we may call the 'just war' tradition. In the very simplest terms (which we shall elaborate later), Christian 'just warriors' accepted the necessity for some war for the sake of maintaining justice between societies, and sought to restrain the practice of war by the requirements of justice. Some saw this necessity in terms of a 'lesser evil'; others believed that war could sometimes be a righteous act to vindicate justice. Justice, all believed, is a necessary condition for true peace.

The minority strand, including many of the early Fathers of the church in the first and second centuries, together with the Waldenses, the Mennonites and the Quakers, has been pacifist. Some of these people would allow some place for the use of force. Others would rule out all force. All were agreed that war is totally against the teaching of

Christ. For them, Christianity is a pacifist faith.

Church history shows how Christians have polarized into these two main traditions of thought. In Chapter 3 we will trace the history of these views in some detail. But first we need to approach the Bible in its own terms and discover what it says about war. We shall need this information in order to make our own assessment of the way Christians in these traditions have thought and argued. Many of the differences between them have derived from different approaches to various examples and various teachings in the Bible. Some of the just warriors have looked to certain Old Testament examples which they believe support the priority of the concern for justice. The New Testament teaching on peace, they say, needs to be read in this light. Many of the pacifists begin rather with the Sermon on the Mount, and seek to approach the Old Testament through a perspective framed by the command to 'love your enemies'.

I hope to show how unsatisfactory it is to try to base our views about war on isolated biblical examples. The theological task is much bigger than that; it will be our concern in Part 3 of this book. But before we can get there, and before we can look more closely at church history, we need to spend some time with the biblical text itself, and to understand the Bible's history and teaching in its own terms. We begin with the Old Testament.

1 Does the Old Testament help?

The Exodus

War, it would seem, was a common experience of the peoples of Old Testament times. As we quickly survey Old Testament history, we find ourselves face to face with a range of situations in which wars are waged and are thought of almost as commonplace.

In the earliest days, when the people of God were desert nomads, there was no distinction between the soldier and the civilian: everyone had to be prepared to defend his tribe's property. It was at the Exodus from Egypt, though, when the people of Israel were constituted a nation under God, that the first picture of a situation resembling war is given. The people of God were in great fear, encamped with the sea in front of them and Pharaoh's horses and chariots marching after them. Moses' word was 'Fear not, stand firm, and see the salvation of the LORD, which he will work for you today . . . the LORD will fight for you, and you have only to be still' (Ex.14:13–14). Then, by miraculous intervention, the waters of the sea were opened, the people of Israel passed through safely and the waters returned and covered the chariots, the horsemen and all the host of Pharaoh. 'Thus the LORD saved Israel that day from the hand of the Egyptians' (Ex.14:30).

Is this the way people of faith are supposed to respond to threat from a heavily armed enemy? To stand still, trust God and wait for the miracle? Many Christian pacifists believe so. God's people display their faith precisely in trusting God in their vulnerability. Victory is assured (though not always in the way expected) because it is God's gift of grace, not the works of man.

Other Christians, however, see the gift of miraculous intervention as an unusual aspect of God's dealings with his people – perhaps a particular encouragement to faith at this early point in the life of the new nation. Certainly there is very little hint elsewhere that this is the way God always plans to work for his people when their security is under threat. We get a different emphasis later in the history of the people of God, particularly at the time of the conquest of Canaan.

The Conquest
The march through the desert towards the land of promise is pictured in terms of an ordered company drawn up in battle array (Nu.1:3; 2:1–31), and on arrival at the land of promise we find the beginnings of wars of conquest and occupation (Nu.21:21–35; 31:1–12; Jos.1–11). There is little sense of a unified armed attack; different tribes seem to take different

territories (Nu.32:1–16, 39–42), although the opening chapter of the book of Joshua depicts a much more ordered national campaign.

One of the perplexing aspects of the accounts of these wars of conquest and occupation, from the point of view of Christian conscience, is that at times they involved considerable massacre, and yet they were associated with the direct command of God. Some Christians have used these narratives as a defence of the view that God sometimes approves of war – even indiscriminate war. Against that we need to set the fact that the sort of warfare described in these chapters is of a very special sort: the 'holy war'.

The wars of Yahweh
We need to be careful in understanding what is meant by 'holy war'. The phrase describes that special sort of war in which the people of God were engaged at the time of the Conquest, and perhaps also at the start of the reign of King David. (The same title is given to the *jihad* in Islamic teaching, but the idea is very different. For the Muslim, a duty is laid on each believer to spread his faith by force of arms. This was an idea picked up by some Christians at the time of the Crusades, and some believe it underlies, for example, some of the events in Northern Ireland in recent days. But the Israelite concept of holy war was very different.) There was no question of spreading the faith by warfare, or indeed defending the faith by warfare. The people were not fighting for God. Rather, God was fighting for his people against those who threatened their existence as the people of God. These wars were God's wars. Some texts speak of 'the wars of Yahweh' (1 Sa.18:17; 25:28); the enemies were the 'enemies of Yahweh' (Jdg.5:31); and reference is made to a no longer extant 'Book of the Wars of Yahweh' (Nu.21:14).

The involvement of the people in the holy war was a participation in what God was doing: it was a cultic act. So special preparations had to be made. The people had to prepare themselves by ritual cleansing (Jos.3:5: 'And Joshua said to the people, "Sanctify yourselves; for tomorrow the LORD will do wonders among you.'"). Before marching out to battle, a sacrifice was offered to Yahweh (1 Sa.7:9) and Yahweh was consulted before the battle was engaged (Jdg.20:27–28; *etc.*). It was Yahweh who decided when his people should go to war, and he himself marched at their head (Jdg.4:14; 2 Sa.5:24).

One of the most illuminating passages concerns the fall of Jericho to Joshua's army, described in Joshua 5:13 – 6:27. It begins with the appearance of the LORD, depicted as 'a man with his drawn sword in his hand'. Joshua asks, '"Are you for us, or for our adversaries?"', to which the 'man' replies – with majesterial sovereignty – '"No; but as commander of the army of the LORD I have now come."' Joshua recognizes that he is in the presence of the LORD, and falls down and worships. Before there is any talk of battle, Joshua acknowledges that the place on which he is standing is holy ground.

After acknowledging God's holiness, Joshua is given a word of promise (6:2), and then details of the plan of campaign (6:3ff.). There is an assurance of victory (6:5), and the word of divine guidance to go before them (6:7). Then, with the ark of the covenant at their head (6:8), symbolizing the presence of the LORD himself, the priests and the people go forward to Jericho and to victory.

The 'devoted things'
A further aspect of the holy war, the victory of which was assured by Yahweh, concerned the *cherem*. This word is often translated 'devoted things' (as in Jos.6:18). It seems to mean that the fruits of victory were to be left only to God: enemy property and goods were not to be taken as booty by the people themselves. This is the reasoning behind the requirement that everything was to be destroyed: everything was to be sacrificed to Yahweh. The spoils of war were his alone. So at Jericho, all living things had to be put to death, and the town burned; the metal objects which would not burn were to be consecrated to Yahweh (Jos.6:18–24).

At other times, the *cherem* ruling was applied less rigorously, but it was almost always commanded by Yahweh (Dt.7:2; 20:17; Jos.8:2; 1 Sa.15:3). So Deuteronomy 7:2–3 tells us that '"when the LORD your God gives them over to you, and you defeat them; then you must utterly destroy them; you shall make no covenant with them, and show no mercy to them. You shall not make marriages with them"'. And why? The reason is given: '"For they would turn away your sons from following me, to serve other gods . . . For you are a people holy to the LORD"' (Dt.7:4,6).

In other words, the holy war, with its associated *cherem* rulings of utter destruction, was concerned with preserving the existence and holiness of the people of Yahweh. At the beginnings of their identity as a people with their own territory, subject to the pressures to conform to the godless peoples around them, the holy war reminded the people that they were the Lord's. Yahweh was their Lord, even in battle. The victories were his alone. The spoils of war must therefore be his alone, and must not be the property of anyone else.

Furthermore, war was decreed by divine command as the means God used to preserve his people against corruption, and even extinction, by the destruction of those who would harm them. The to us almost incomprehensibly severe conduct of the holy war was thus to protect Israel's existence as a holy people, holy to the Lord. It served also to remind her of her dependence on Yahweh for all things: she was saved by 'his great works'.

It would seem very dubious, therefore, to argue from so specialized a concept of warfare associated with a people at the very beginnings of their national identity as the people of God, to any general view that 'God approves of war', let alone 'God sanctions indiscriminate warfare'. It is even less clear how links could be made from the example of a theocratic nation whose national identity was bound up with their calling to be God's holy people, to decisions concerning war between modern sovereign states. (The holy war does, however, point in these writings to one aspect of the character of

God which later writers further elaborate, namely that in certain circumstances he does order a judgment against evil which is both dreadful and destructive.) It is on such biblical examples that some Christian writers have sought to build a case for the justice of war, even indiscriminate war.

The growth of militarism

At the times of the Conquest, we have said, Israel was engaged in offensive wars of occupation. Under the later times of the Judges, there were military campaigns, but almost entirely defensive ones, to protect Israel's existence as a people. This pattern continued under the kingship of Saul, but when David became king, there was a return for a while to a policy of military and territorial expansion. This did not last long, and there was scarcely any warfare during Solomon's reign. After the division of the kingdom, there were a number of border conflicts, though not many, but these were primarily defensive ones aimed at bringing back dependent territory, keeping a trade route open, or protecting a frontier.

With the establishment of the kingdom, however, an important change had occurred in the people's understanding of war. The concept of the holy war as it had been understood at the time of the Conquest, was giving way to something else. The people had called for a king in order to be 'like the nations' around. And as kingship became established in the life of the people of God, so the state became consolidated under the established authority of the king. The people of God viewed themselves less now as a theocracy under the direction of the charismatic leader inspired by God, and more as a monarchy with an earthly ruler. There seem to have been moves to establish a professional army: Saul's mercenaries (1 Sa.14:52), directly under the rule of the king (1 Sa.23:25–26), were used against the Philistines (1 Sa.18:27). An army of paid soldiers was established under the rule of David (2 Sa.5:6, *etc.*). A chariot force was built up under Solomon (1 Ki.10:28–29), which was quartered in

Jerusalem (2 Ki.11:16) and in various 'chariot cities' (1 Ki. 10:26, *etc.*). And very much later there seems also on occasion to have been a small cavalry (*e.g.* 1 Macc.16:4).

So the idea of a man being called to arms by a charismatic leader inspired by God, to fight in God's holy war, thus gave way during the monarchy to a mobilization of troops under the command of the king (2 Ki.3:7). The curious episode of the census recorded in 2 Samuel 24:1–9 is instructive here. The sort of men chosen to do the census shows us its military character. Was David's concern to establish some human organization of the people for military purposes, and did he do so in a way which represented a wrongful intrusion by man's authority into an area which hitherto had been the prerogative of God himself? Joab certainly thought so, and David himself eventually came to realize that he was wrong to have taken the census. The king's concern with human manpower and human organization was a departure from the pattern of God's rule. We remember the smallness of the group and the faithful dependence only on God seen, for example, in the exploits of Gideon against the Midianites. Was David's action an abandonment of the idea of Yahweh's war – a decision to see warfare in terms only of political necessity, and not in terms also of the holy war of Yahweh? We may perhaps judge that it was. Whatever our conclusion, however, it is hard to see how David's experiences can give clear guidelines for our political and moral decisions.

War as God's judgment

The idea that 'the battle is the LORD's' was not altogether lost. It was alive in the consciousness of the people even as late as 2 Chronicles 20:15. Men of faith held on to the view that God was their divine warrior (Ps.24:8). The title 'Yahweh of hosts' depicts Yahweh as commander of all powers, supernatural as well as the natural, of the army of Israel. Indeed the later prophets can still appeal to the holy war idea as a basis for their message. But they often do so in terms of criticism of the king and people. The holy war was meant to be an expression of humble dependence on God. What was happening rather was that the people were claiming that God was with them as he always had been, although in reality they were organizing their own military strategies.

So a decisively different note is struck in some of the prophetic writings. If God's people abandon his sovereign rule, Yahweh, the divine warrior, will do battle not *for* Israel, but *against* them! Israel have departed from the ways of Yahweh, so future wars will be expressions of divine judgment. Indeed, some of the prophets predict the downfall of the people of Israel altogether, apart from a small faithful remnant who remain true to their God, and in whom the true Israel still lives on.

In the eighth century BC, for example, Amos (2:6–12) reminds the people of Israel of their sins of social injustice and disobedience to God's holy law, that his holy name is profaned among them. Yet, says Amos, referring to Joshua 9–10, it was Yahweh who destroyed the Amorites before them (Am.2:9), as part of that holy war intended to preserve his holy name among his holy people. Because of their sin, God's people have now forfeited their right to call Yahweh the God who fights for them: he will instead be against them (Am.2:13ff.).

At the later time of the reign of Josiah, the prophet Jeremiah interprets the signs of the times in terms of God's coming judgment. War will no longer be the war of Yahweh fighting for his people. It will be the judgment of Yahweh against his people who have turned away from him:

Declare in Judah, and proclaim in Jerusalem, and say, 'Blow the trumpet through the land; cry aloud and say, "Assemble, and let us go into the fortified cities!" Raise a standard toward Zion, flee for safety, stay not, for I bring evil from the north, and great destruction' (Je.4:5–6).

God's people had not discerned the signs of the times; men

had been lulled into a false sense of security; they had not taken seriously the real nature of their God; they had failed to repent of their faithlessness. Now God's judgment would no longer be held back.

Later we read Jeremiah's vivid description of the horrors of war:

'Who will have pity on you, O Jerusalem, or who will
    bemoan you?
Who will turn aside to ask about your welfare?
You have rejected me, says the LORD, you keep going
    backward;
so I have stretched out my hand against you and destroyed
    you;—
I am weary of relenting.
I have winnowed them with a winnowing fork in the gates
    of the land;
I have bereaved them, I have destroyed my people; they
    did not turn from their ways.
I have made their widows more in number than the sand
    of the seas;
I have brought against the mothers of young men a
    destroyer at noonday;
I have made anguish and terror fall upon them suddenly.
She who bore seven has languished; she has swooned
    away; her sun went down while it was yet day; she has
    been shamed and disgraced.
And the rest of them I will give to the sword before their
    enemies,' says the LORD (Je.15:5–9).

Thankfully, there is eventually some relief in the prophetic lament for his wayward countrymen, and the picture later is of the war of God not against Israel, but against Babylon, because of their wickedness against God's people (Je.51:1–5). Ultimately, Israel and Judah are not forsaken by their God (51:5a). But in the above quotation from chapter 15, we have the prophet's anguished lament for a people who have wearied God beyond the point of repentance, and against whom war is to be waged as God's judgment upon them.

War – quite apart from its fearful political reality – has also become a symbol.

From the much earlier days of Amos, in fact, this symbolic aspect of war has been implicit, although not until Jeremiah does it reach such forceful and sustained expression. But even in Amos, the Coming Day of the Lord is associated with terrible wars (Am.5–7). Likewise in the Southern Kingdom, Isaiah speaks of the desolation and destruction which accompanies the Day of the Lord (Is.13:6ff.). Much later also the prophet Joel, while on the one hand foretelling the renewal of Judah and Jerusalem, also prophesies judgment on the nations around:

> Proclaim this among the nations: Prepare war, stir up the mighty men. Let all the men of war draw near, let them come up. Beat your ploughshares into swords, and your pruning hooks into spears; let the weak say, 'I am a warrior.' . . . Bring down thy warriors, O Lord (Joel 3:9–11).

In war as a symbol of God's judgment, we find an Old Testament theme which stands in marked contrast to those other strands of the Old Testament which, as we have seen, some Christians have interpreted as justification of war. God is the warrior against evil, to be sure. He at times orders a judgment against evil which is dreadful and destructive – a premise which some Christian pacifist writers seek to deny or forget. God in the Old Testament is not always against war as such.

But whose side is he on? That is a further disturbing question. There is an ambiguity in the way God's warfare against evil is translated into national political decisions. Is God for his people, or is he acting in judgment on their sins? It needs the specific word of the prophet to discern the activity of God in any political scenario. Again, this should warn us that specific Old Testament examples are quite inconclusive for today's Christian questions. We cannot build our theology of war on isolated Old Testament examples. One of our tasks for today's world is to discern the Lord's voice, and to speak the prophetic word for our day.

The triumph of the Coming One

Alongside, but again in contrast with, this strong symbolic understanding of war as a vehicle for the judgment of God against evil, there is another prophetic emphasis. In the latter days, things will be different. The day will come, say the prophets, when there will be universal peace. This peace will spread between nation and nation, between man and man, between man and the rest of the created order. This is another theme we can trace from as early as the eighth century BC (Is.2:2–4, cf. Mi.4:1–4). We find it also in the later word of Zechariah: the day will come when the Lord will be king over all the earth, and Jerusalem will dwell in peace (Zc.14:9–11).

The early vision of Messiah's rule of peace (Is.11:1–10) is one side of the prophetic emphasis. The other finds expression in Zephaniah's vision of the eventual victory of the Lord: 'The LORD, your God, is in your midst, a warrior who gives victory' (Zp.3:17). Here is a vision to sustain the people of God!

The picture of Yahweh as the divine warrior who brings peace in eventual triumph over all his enemies was kept alive in the apocalyptic literature of post-exilic days. After the exile, Israel was a small religious group with very little political autonomy. There were the wars of independence under Judas Maccabaeus in 165 BC, but very little other military activity. However, the apocalyptic writings kept alive the vision of the triumph of the Coming One:

> I saw in the night visions, and behold, with the clouds of heaven there came one like a son of man, and he came to the Ancient of Days and was presented before him. And to him was given dominion and glory and kingdom, that all peoples, nations, and languages should serve him; his

dominion is an everlasting dominion, which shall not pass away, and his kingdom one that shall not be destroyed (Dn.7:13f.).

The Old Testament, then, pictures war in a variety of different contexts. God sometimes fights for his people, sometimes against them in judgment. War is sometimes his command, sometimes his weapon. There is a movement in the faith of the people from reliance on the God of miracle to the use of their own military might in the Lord's service.

Throughout all the variety, the character of God's holy love remains a constant factor. God requires his people to 'do justice, and to love kindness, and to walk humbly with your God' (Mi.6:8).

While affirming the Old Testament faith in Yahweh as the warrior against evil, we must be very cautious about relating any particular Old Testament examples of warfare directly to our very different world.

2 Is the New Testament conclusive?

Gospel allusions to military service

When we turn from the Old Testament to the New we find a picture which in social and political terms is very different. In the Gospels, the political background is the Roman occupation of the land of Palestine, with evidence of a growing Zealot movement of rebellion.

There are three particular allusions to war or military service in the Gospels, all in Luke. In Luke 3:14 some soldiers, presumably on active service, asked John the Baptist what they should do in response to his preaching of repentance and the coming of the Lord. The Baptist replies: 'Rob no one by violence or by false accusation, and be content with your wages.' In line with his words to the multitudes and to the tax collectors, John does not tell the soldiers to leave their profession, but in the context of their work as soldiers to express their response by turning their backs on greed and by appropriate submission to authority.

In Luke 14:31, Jesus is recorded as expounding the importance of counting the cost of discipleship by using the analogy of a king taking stock of his resources before going to war. War is neither commended nor condemned; rather it is taken for granted.

Thirdly, in a remarkable paragraph in Luke 19:41ff., we read of Jesus with tears in his eyes, looking ahead to the war which will destroy Jerusalem.

'And when he drew near and saw the city he wept over it, saying, "Would that . . . you knew the things that make for peace!"' Then come these strong words of judgment: '"For the days shall come upon you, when your enemies will cast up a bank about you and surround you, and hem you in on every side, and dash you to the ground, you and your children within you, and they will not leave one stone upon another in you; because you did not know the time of your visitation."'

The tears are the tears of God when he sees the pain and suffering caused by foolish refusal of his kingly rule; Jerusalem fell to the Romans in AD 70.

Elsewhere in the New Testament, apart from the apocalyptic passages in the book of Revelation, warfare between man and man is barely mentioned. Military personnel do feature in the Gospels and the Acts of the Apostles in particular, however. We meet the centurion from Capernaum with the paralysed servant (Mt.8:5ff.); the soldiers of the governor who marched Jesus to the cross (Mt.27:27); the centurion at the cross (Mk.15:39); the military presence in Jerusalem (Acts 21:31ff.; 22:25); the praetorian guard standing custody over Paul (Phil.1:13); and others besides. Military service seems to be taken for granted as a fact of life.

Causes of wars

But what causes wars? One New Testament writer looks at that question directly. At the close of James chapter 3, the author discusses the relationship between righteousness and peace, concluding with the difficult verse 18: '. . . the harvest of righteousness is sown in peace by those who make peace.' This could mean two things. Either it could mean that peace is one of the results of righteousness – a fact which the Bible often indicates (as for example in Is.32:17: '. . . the effect of righteousness will be peace, and the result of righteousness, quietness and trust for ever'). Or it could mean that the righteousness which God demands cannot be achieved by man's 'jealousy and selfish ambition' (verse 16), but is rather a harvest of the seed that is 'sown in peace by those who make peace'. Calvin comments on this verse that 'they who study peace, are nevertheless careful to sow righteousness; nor are they slothful or negligent in promoting and encouraging good works; but they moderate their zeal with the condiment of peace.' And again: 'those who wish to be physicians to heal vices ought not to be executioners.'[1] Either way, the state of true blessedness is found when 'righteousness and peace will kiss each other' (Ps.85:10).

It is in this context that James then exposes the attitudes and impulses in human nature which prevent the establishment of such a state of righteous peace and peaceful righteousness:

> What causes wars, and what causes fightings among you?
> Is it not your passions that are at war in your members?
> You desire and do not have; so you kill. And you covet
> and cannot obtain; so you fight and wage war (Jas.4:1–2).

Most commentators take 'war', in the context of this letter written to Christian people, to refer primarily to personal quarrelling within the community, but the reasons James gives are no less valid on the national scale. Strife and disorder within the human heart are among the dominant characteristics of human life. The seeds of strife are found in the hearts and minds of men and women. Human 'passions' are 'at war' within.

Paul uses a very similar word in Romans 7:23: '. . . I see in my members another law at war with the law of my mind and making me captive to the law of sin'. As Tasker put it: 'The human personality has been invaded by an alien army which is always campaigning within it.'[2]

Killing is the result of thwarted desires. James underlines what can and does happen when human life is lived according to principles of selfish covetousness and greed to the exclusion of the 'wisdom from above'. As Mitton comments: 'This is not other than our Lord warned us to be prepared for. He said "For from within, out of the heart of man, comes . . . murder" (Mk.7:21). The Old Testament bears witness to the same grim truth. Bitter jealousy led Cain to kill Abel. Thwarted covetousness led to Naboth's death at the hands of Ahab and Jezebel. Uriah the Hittite was sent to his death to make way for David's lust.'[3] Quarrels, murders and wars begin in the minds and hearts of men.

Conflict with evil

Although the world of the New Testament was socially and politically very different from that of the Old, there is continuity between the Testaments in the assumption of a background of conflict between God and the powers of evil. To be sure, the New Testament no longer sees the people of God in terms of national identity. The enemies of God are no longer equated with the enemies of Israel. But through the New Testament runs a strong strand of teaching concerning the warfare between the holy God and the powers of evil, and this underlay much of Jesus' life and ministry.

The prophet Simeon spoke of the 'fall and rising of many in Israel' through the birth of Jesus, and of a sword that would pierce Mary's own soul also (Lk.2:34–35). In his ministry, 'Jesus when confronted with suffering and pain in others invariably shows himself the fighter'[4] – whether the enemy be death, or the demonic, or disease, or the storm. Jesus even describes himself as a man of war in this sense: '"Do not think that I have come to bring peace on earth; I have not come to bring peace, but a sword"' (Mt.10:34), meaning that Jesus will cause division between people: men will be separated from one another by their responses to him. Jesus sees his ministry in terms of binding the power of Satan (Mk.3:23ff.), and indeed the road to the cross begins with the conflict with Satan in the wilderness (Mt.4:1ff.), and goes by way of the place where, in opposition to the words of Satan, Jesus teaches that the Son of Man must suffer and be killed (Mk.8:31–33). One of the primary strands of New Testament teaching concerning the atonement (classically stated by G. Aulen in *Christus Victor*) is that in the cross God has 'disarmed the principalities and powers ... triumphing over them' in Christ (*cf*. Col.2:15), and that in the death and resurrection of Christ, Death itself is swallowed up in victory (1 Cor. 15:54).

'Love your enemies'
In the context of the conflict of Christ with the powers of evil and the establishment of the kingly rule of God in the hearts of men, it is all the more poignant to recall the matchless teaching of the life of the kingdom given in the Sermon on the Mount. In particular, Matthew 5:38–48 stand as the manifesto for Christian pacifism: 'Do not resist one who is evil'; 'love your enemies'.

There is considerable difference of opinion among Christian commentators concerning the interpretation of the Sermon on the Mount in general, and these antitheses in Matthew 5 in particular. Are we dealing simply with ethical demands separated from the context of the Gospel (as some liberal humanists would interpret the sayings), or with extreme ethical demands for the end-time (as those who think that Jesus was expecting the imminent end of all things would argue)? Is this the statement of counsels of perfection, set before us as impossible ideals? Or is the teaching meant to be taken absolutely at face value as specific commands for Christian behaviour? Many of those who argue in this last way would also want to insist that the Sermon on the Mount is meant to be applied not only to Christian believers in their personal relationships, but as a rule governing social relationships as well. This would take us into the realm of practical Christian politics, as the Anabaptist-Mennonite tradition believes. Most commentators in the Reformed traditions, on the other hand, believe that the antitheses of the Sermon serve as particular illustrations of the radical demands of discipleship in the kingdom; they bring out the true but often obscured meaning of the Old Testament torah, but they need to be understood in the light of the rest of Scripture also.

We will ourselves need to spend much more time on this material, and on the relationship between personal and political ethics, when we turn back to these verses in Chapter 7.

The cleansing of the temple

In the paragraphs in John 2:15ff. and Mark 11:15ff. we are given an example of Jesus' apparent use of force against evil which is sometimes used as an argument against Christian pacifism. However, the relevance of this text to Christian discussions of warfare is not unambiguous. On the one hand, some Christian pacifists argue that the 'scourge' which Jesus used was in all probability for the sheep and the goats, and that it was the authority of Jesus' word which sent out the traders. The motivation behind Jesus' action was that the temple was meant to be 'a house of prayer for all the nations' (Mk.11:17). It would then be possible to read this incident as a plea from Jesus on behalf of the Gentiles who were being prevented from approach to Israel's God by this misuse of the temple court. Rather than sanctioning war, this is an appeal to international mutual care.

On the other hand, John's account (unlike those of the other Gospel writers) appears at the opening of Jesus' ministry, immediately after his manifestation of divine glory at

Cana. In Jesus' strong, physical reaction to the misuse of the house of prayer, God is cleansing his own temple in a quite decisive act of judgment.

The 'swords' sayings

Two paragraphs which cause some difficulty for interpreters concern Jesus' references to the sword. In Luke 22:36–38, Jesus says: '"But now, let him who has a purse take it, and likewise a bag. And let him who has no sword sell his mantle and buy one. For I tell you that this scripture must be fulfilled in me, 'And he was reckoned with transgressors'; for what is written about me has its fulfilment." And they said, "Look, Lord, here are two swords." And he said to them, "It is enough."' What is going on here?

This teaching appears to contrast starkly with Jesus' later reaction in the Garden of Gethsemane when he rebukes the disciple who reaches for his sword to protect his master and cuts off the ear of the high priest's slave (Lk.22:51). '"Put your sword back into its place; for all who take the sword will perish by the sword."'

How are these two paragraphs to be understood?

The setting of the first of these paragraphs in the Gospel of Luke is at the point of separation between the Master and his followers. In their earlier ministry, Jesus asked them to recall (Lk.22:35), they had been sent out without purse or bag or sandals, and they had been well received and provided for by those to whom they preached. But now everything is going to be different. From now on Jesus will not be with them in the same way. As his followers, they are going to have to expect rejection, persecution, hostility. They can no longer depend on the generosity of others; they will be on their own in a hostile world. The most likely interpretation of the reference to the 'sword', therefore, is that given by Geldenhuys: 'They must, the Saviour declares in a striking figure, as his followers in the struggle of life, be just as determined and whole-hearted as a fighting man who gives up everything, even his garment, as long as he only possesses a sword to continue the struggle with.'[5] In other words, this is a graphic way of saying to the disciples that they are in a situation of grave peril. The sword is a symbolic way of expressing the difficulties they will face.

On this interpretation, the reply of the disciples then can be seen as their continuing lack of realization of the spiritual nature of Jesus' work. They take his reference to the sword literally, and say that there are two of them available. Jesus then replies, 'It is enough', meaning not 'Two swords will be sufficient', but rather 'Enough of this kind of talk!' Jesus' later reference to the sword in verse 51 in his rebuke to the disciple who cut off the servant's ear, means 'that the use of the sword is not lawful in the defence of His cause'.[6]

An alternative interpretation of the first sword passage sees the sword, along with the purse and the bag, as necessary equipment for the traveller. In country infested with bandits and robbers, the sword may be a symbol and means of legitimate self-defence. This approach would solve the problem of the association of this word in this paragraph with Jesus' impending arrest and death, and leave us with the refusal to use the sword in the garden. But perhaps this suggests that while Jesus may allow for legitimate self-defence, it is an altogether different thing to rely on the power of the sword. Either way, there is no basis in this passage for a justification for the use of the sword in the cause of the kingdom of God.

Christian warfare

Whatever we decide to do with the difficult 'swords' sayings in the Gospels, we need be in no doubt that many of the New Testament authors describe the Christian life in terms of warfare. We are to 'put on the whole armour of God' in order to stand against the wiles of the devil (Eph.6:11ff.). We are not contending against flesh and blood, but against 'the principalities, against the powers, against the world rulers of this present darkness, against the spiritual hosts of wickedness in the heavenly places'. Timothy is told to 'wage the good warfare' (1 Tim.1:18), holding faith and a good conscience; he is to 'fight the good fight of the faith' (1 Tim.6:12). He is to take his share of suffering as a 'good soldier of Jesus Christ' (2 Tim.2:3f.); and Paul, towards the end of his life, says of himself that he has 'fought the good fight' (2 Tim.4:7).

There is a note of confidence in this faith: we are 'more than conquerors' (Rom.8:37); God gives us the 'victory' (1 Cor.15:57); 'this is the victory which overcomes the world, our faith' (1 Jn.5:4). And in the vivid apocalyptic imagery of the book of Revelation, we see that behind all the struggles of the Christian church there stands the heavenly warrior, Christ himself, Captain of the armies of heaven. 'In righteousness he judges and makes war' says Revelation 19:11, with the suggestion that the heavenly armies are being led out now in the history of the church on earth, to fight against evil and to bring men to the judgment of decision. 'There is one war and one victory which the followers of the Messiah have to repeat in their own lives. By his weapons, which are his own blood of sacrifice, and the sword of the Word of God (cf. Ps.45:3ff.), he continues to wage war until he secures both the overcoming of the world empires (Rev.17:14) and the ultimate destruction of evil (Rev.20:7–10; cf. 2 Thes.2:8ff.).'[7] There is no 'holy war' in a political sense in the New Testament. There is rather the 'spiritual warfare' of the people of God. Their weapons are the blood of sacrifice and the sword of the Spirit.

We have completed our survey of the way the Bible speaks of war and uses the language of war. In the Old Testament histories, sometimes God fights for his faithful people, securing their existence. Sometimes he fights against his faithless people in judgment on their sin. In the New Testament we see Jesus showing us a God who confronts evil, yet his own teaching and example also demonstrate how that confrontation needs to be related to costly love for enemies. We will have to come back to this relation in a later chapter. Likewise, the Christian life is described as a warfare, but the weapons are spiritual.

What bearing all this has on present Christian attitudes to war in our day we will explore in a later chapter. We do well, however, to notice the difficulty this varied picture gives us in finding any unambiguous examples for today's political scene. This is not to say that the Bible is of no relevance: far from it. It is rather to raise the question *how* the Bible is to be used in making moral and political decisions. What does not change is the character of God. That Christ is at war with evil is unmistakably clear. But the ways appropriate for the expression of this character in social, political and national terms are many and varied.

I shall argue in much more detail in Part 3 that we need to place these biblical examples in a broad theological framework which itself is derived from the biblical witness. We come to the Bible through our own sets of assumptions and theological presuppositions. We must allow the Bible to call these in question, and dictate for us its own theological parameters. Through that theological task, to which we will later turn our attention, we will perhaps be able more clearly to interpret this varied map of biblical examples, and also the varied and complex issues of today's world.

Before we do this, however, we pause to ask what other Christians have said about war, and try to learn from the traditions of the church some of the theological issues about which we shall need to form our own judgments. It is to church history, therefore, that we now turn.

Notes for chapter two

[1]J. Calvin, *Commentaries on the Catholic Epistles* (tr. J. Owen, 1855), commentary on James 3:16.

[2]R. V. G. Tasker, *The General Epistle of James* (Tyndale Press, 1957), p.85.

[3]C. L. Mitton, *The Epistle of James* (Marshall, Morgan & Scott, 1966), p.148.

[4]F. D. Coggan, *Convictions* (Hodder & Stoughton, 1975), p.274.

[5]J. N. Geldenhuys, *Commentary on the Gospel of Luke* (Marshall, Morgan & Scott, 1950).

[6]*Ibid.*

[7]C. F. Evans, 'War' in A. Richardson (ed.), *Theological Word Book of the Bible* (SCM, 1957), p.277.

3 Historical sketch

One of the tools for Christian moral decision-making is the resource of the Christian church. How have other Christians made up their minds? In order to learn from them, we turn our attention now to the witness of Christian tradition. Or, rather, Christian traditions, because – as we have said – there has in fact been a long history of disagreement between Christians as to whether or not the taking up of arms in war is compatible with Christian faith.

We need constantly to bear in mind as we go on that, just as we cannot transpose the biblical material directly into our own times, as though it were written in response to our questions, so we cannot lift the teaching of theologians of an earlier age and apply it directly to our own. Their social and political situations were very different from ours. War for some of them meant a very personal confrontation between leaders. For some, words like 'chivalry' in war were of highest importance. Some could see issues clearly in terms of black and white. Few could have envisaged the possibilities of destruction the world has seen this century. None even poses the question of total global war, such as is now on our own agenda.

On the other hand, we must not write off Christian traditions as of no value. We must try to learn how Christians of an earlier age made up their minds on the issues facing them in the light of their faith in God. We will try to learn from them the theological principles which mattered to them in their answers to their questions. And we shall try to use this to help us frame our questions and move towards answers for our own very different needs.

What follows is a brief historical sketch. A full picture is of course beyond the scope of this book's aim.

The early church
The weight of Christian opinion in the first three centuries of

35

the Christian era was opposed to the idea that Christians could participate in military service. The reasons for this were partly political and social, and partly theological.

On the political and social side, we need to remember that in its earliest days the Christian church would have been viewed by the Roman occupying power as a radical sect within Judaism, and the Romans forbade Jews to engage in service with the imperial army (except as a punishment in some circumstances). Christians came into contact with the military, therefore, primarily as the army acted as agent of the Emperor's persecution of Christians. There is evidence of great brutality and cruelty being shown by many soldiers towards Christians in the early decades. There is little likelihood that a Christian would have chosen to be a soldier, had that been possible. The problem of conscientious objection to military service may have arisen occasionally for those Roman soldiers who converted to the Christian faith, but this was not widespread in the first two centuries. Furthermore, the Roman army was officially committed to the cult of Emperor worship, with an obligatory oath of allegiance laid on the soldiers. On grounds of idolatry, therefore, few Christians would have felt able to act as soldiers for the Emperor, even if their professional prospects for doing so had been good.

It was not only the political situation, however, that led to the refusal of Christians to enlist in military service. There were theological issues at stake as well. The Christian had to decide where his loyalties lay in the context of an idolatrous pagan state. On the one hand he was opposed to the cult of Emperor worship. On the other hand, some parts of the New Testament (*e.g.* Rom.13:1ff.) seemed to indicate that loyalty to the state was a Christian duty. Was this Roman state really the 'servant of God' of which Paul had written? Or was it nearer the demonic picture of Revelation chapter 13? Many Christian writers came to see the state as having a limited role under God. They held firmly also to the fact that this life is not all that there is. The Christian is a citizen of two cities, an earthly and a heavenly. He needed therefore to hold in tension in his mind the positive approach to the state of Paul in Romans 13 and the negative, demonic picture of the book of Revelation. We will ourselves need to look at this further in a later chapter (Chapter 10).

This meant that many early Christians felt free to refuse to serve the state when it required idolatrous Emperor worship, and would not therefore have enlisted for the army. Their pacifism was part of their non-engagement with a society they judged alien to their Christian faith. Furthermore, many of the early Christians believed that in any case military service was incompatible with the Christian gospel of love. Jesus had taught 'Love your enemies'; it could not be part of a Christian's vocation to kill them.

But, we may ask, what is the relation between the gospel of love and the apparent acceptance of war by this same God in the Old Testament? And what about the military metaphors used to describe the Christian life in the New Testament epistles? How did the early church handle questions such as these?

Some of the early Fathers of the church made a firm separation between the Old Testament and the New. The expression of faith under the law was now radically altered, it was believed, under the dispensation of grace. Most still cherished the Old Testament as a reminder of the holy justice of God, and as the history of the covenant people leading up to the coming of Christ (although some, following Marcion, rejected the Old Testament altogether). But now this had to be reinterpreted for the Christian conscience in the light of the law of love which the New Testament made clear.

The continuing value of the Old Testament for the Christian thus lay in its *spiritual*, not literal, meaning. There was consequently a considerable amount of allegorical, symbolic and 'spiritualizing' interpretations of the Old Testament by many of the early Fathers. The military metaphors of the New Testament were frequently used, but never as a justification of military service. They were seen rather as vivid descriptions of the Christian's spiritual conflict, especially in prayer. In a comment on the patristic age, J. M. Hornus writes:

> The Christians, by interpreting the whole Bible in the light of the law of love which had been most clearly revealed in the gospel, could use the military narratives and bellicose expressions while at the same time disarming them of their brutal character. They knew that their battle was a real one. But it took place on a different plane, and with quite different weapons, from the battles of the world.[1]

Let us look at some examples of the writings of these times. Some Christians believed that all bloodshed, whether by soldiers or executioners, was incompatible with the gospel. At one stage the Church of Alexandria looked askance at receiving soldiers into membership. The church historian K. Latourette writes: 'Hippolytus, prominent in Rome, in putting down in writing what he believed to be the apostolic tradition and so the authentic Christian teaching, maintained that when he applied for admission to the Christian fellowship, a soldier must refuse to kill men even if he were commanded by his superiors to do so . . . a catechumen or baptized person who sought to enlist as a soldier must be cut off from the Church.'[2]

Tertullian (c. AD 160–230) argued against a Christian being a member of the Roman armies on the ground that this brought him under a master other than Christ, that it entailed taking the sword, and that even when the army was used as a police force in peace time, it made the infliction of punishment necessary, which was forbidden to the Christian. In disarming Peter, said Tertullian, Christ had unbelted every soldier.

> If we are enjoined then to love our enemies, whom have we to hate? If injured we are forbidden to retaliate, lest we

become as bad ourselves. In our religion it is counted better to be slain than to slay.[3]

For Tertullian there can be no engagement in army religion – and hence idolatry. Not only soldiery, but any civil enforcement of punishment is forbidden the Christian. We can judge something of the strength of opposition of the early Christians to military service from the fact that Celsus made this one of his points of attack against Christians. If all were to behave as Christians did, he argued, the Empire would fall to the barbarians. Origen's (AD 184–254) famous reply argued rather that if all were to become Christians, the barbarians would also be Christians, and that even though Christians were at present in a minority, they were doing more by their love and prayers to preserve the Empire than ever the Roman armies were. Origen writes:

> The Christian lawgiver nowhere teaches that it is right for his own disciples to offer violence to any one, however wicked, or to allow the killing of any individual whatever. Christians have adopted laws of so exceedingly mild a character as not to allow them to resist their persecutors . . . For we no longer take up a 'sword against nation' nor do we 'learn war any more', having become children of peace.[4]

Perhaps the most extreme statement comes from Lactantius in the early fourth century:

> When God forbids us to kill, it will be neither lawful for a just man to engage in warfare . . . nor to accuse anyone of a capital charge, since it is the act of putting to death itself which is prohibited. With regard to this precept there ought to be no exception at all; it is always unlawful to put to death a man, whom God willed to be a sacred animal.[5]

Lactantius, in fact, was soon to change his mind with the

39

emergence of Constantine. His later work praises the Emperor for his Christian victories.

Onwards from Constantine

For the first two centuries, Christian pacifism was largely theoretical, and there was little pressure to serve in the army. It was a pacifism that was largely religious and not ethical. In the third century, however, numbers of Roman soldiers were converted to the Christian faith, and the issue became more pressing and more practical. It reached a watershed when the Emperor Constantine converted to the Christian faith, and made Christianity the official religion of the Roman Empire (AD 313 onwards). The church then had carefully to rethink again its attitude to military service. Lactantius, as we said, changed his attitude. Eusebius celebrated the victories of Constantine as victories of God. The approach of many Christians to war changed considerably. The cross now even became a military emblem. In AD 314 the Synod of Arles gave freedom to Christians to serve in the army. Through the writings of Ambrose, Bishop of Milan (AD 340–397), the predominant pacifism of the first three centuries was changed into an acceptance by the Christian conscience of the need for war in some circumstances, provided it be just. Ambrose praises Joshua, Jerubbaal, Samson and David, 'ready to fight for God and for their rights'; he commended 'fortitude in war', and the attitude that was ready to prefer death to slavery or disgrace. However, says Ambrose, justice must be preserved in all dealings with enemies, and the conquered must be dealt with in a humane manner. Ambrose did not think that priests should participate in war: it is 'foreign to the duty of our office'. In a significant shift of emphasis, it is in the context of *individual* relationships that Christians must not return violence with violence. 'When he meets with an armed robber, he cannot return his blows lest in defending his life he should stain his love towards his neighbour.'[6]

Here are the beginnings of a Christian exposition of what

has come to be called the 'just war theory'. The seeds of this are found in some of the pre-Christian classical thinkers, particularly Cicero, but it was Ambrose and then Augustine who established this tradition within the conscience of the Christian church. Ambrose said, 'I consider that, in the matter of war, care must be taken to see whether wars are just or unjust.'[7] This was not intended in any sense as a justification of war. It was an acknowledgment that not all wars are just. However, the surrender of principles and the toleration of the tyranny of evil could sometimes be judged to be a greater evil than the evil of war. The war that is claimed to be just is one which resists evil and defends righteousness and freedom.

It was through Augustine (AD 354–430) that the theory of 'just war' became firmly established in Christian thinking. He wrote at a time when the state and the church had merged together, and when it had become a common practice for Christians to fight behind the emblem of the cross on a military banner. Augustine lived during the barbarian invasions of the Empire, and he died in Carthage when that city was under siege. He wrote to Boniface, the defender of Carthage at that time, that war is sometimes a matter of necessity in a sinful world. 'Do not think that it is impossible for anyone to please God while engaged in active military service. ... Peace is not sought in order to the kindling of war, but war is waged in order that peace may be obtained. Therefore even in waging war cherish the spirit of a peacemaker, that by conquering those whom you attack, you may lead them back to the advantages of peace. ... Let necessity, and not your will, slay the enemy who fights against you. As violence is used towards him who rebels and resists, so mercy is due to the vanquished or the captive, especially in the case in which future troubling of the peace is not to be feared.'[8]

Whereas Augustine longed for peace, he believed both that it is impossible for governments not to use force against invaders as against criminals, and also that perfect peace is

41

reserved for heaven. As with Ambrose, Augustine made the key distinction between state and individual moral action. He upheld the personal ethics of the Sermon on the Mount: 'The private citizen may not defend himself because he cannot do so without passion and a loss of love. . . . As to killing to defend one's own life, I do not approve, unless one happens to be a soldier or a public functionary acting in defence of others or of the city.' However, despite this individual pacifism, Augustine believed that the defence of what is right in the cause of others, the cause of the state, the cause of God's purposes, may allow a Christian to make military service a Christian vocation. Clergy and monks, however, were to be entirely exempt.[9]

It is largely from Augustine that the continuing 'just war tradition' in Christian thinking stems.

In Augustine several elements receive strong emphasis: 'Righteous wars may be defined as wars to avenge wrongs, when a State has to be attacked for neglecting either to make reparation for misdeeds committed by its citizens, or to restore what has been wrongfully seized. A just peace is always desirable, and war may be legitimate to secure it, to reduce injustice. War should be waged only as necessity, and that through it God may deliver men from necessity and preserve them in peace. Even in war, the spirit of the peacemaker must be cherished. Just wars may include wars to defend safety, to avenge injuries, or in face of refusal to grant passage. To be 'just' war must be waged only by the proper state authority; and its conduct must be just – keeping faith with the enemy, fulfilling promises, avoiding unnecessary violence, looting, massacre, vengeance, atrocities, reprisals. The temptations of the military life – especially to vengefulness and hate – must be met by deep personal devotion.'[10]

There are three significant differences between the approach of Augustine and that of the earlier Fathers, to which we shall have to give our own attention in due course:

First, Augustine believed that the state may sometimes do

what it would be wrong for a private individual to do. This raises the question for us of the relation of the Christian to the state.

Second, Augustine's view of sin led him to see war as sometimes a tragic necessity for the sake of justice. How does the Christian view of the law of love relate to the reality of evil in the world? Can war really be abolished this side of heaven?

Third, Augustine refers to the Old Testament warrior heroes like Joshua as a basis for commending the quest for justice, and the rightness of the people of God in standing against evil. How does the Old Testament view of the conflict of God against evil mesh with the gospel of love?

The Middle Ages and the Medieval Church

Augustine's influence became widespread, but the more pacific strand in Christian thinking was not altogether lost, and perhaps found expression in the fact that those Christian soldiers who had killed in war were obliged to do long terms of penance when they returned. With the break-up of the Empire, however, new features began to emerge and become prominent. The end of the ninth century was a time of deep darkness in the church in the West – indeed for Western Europe as a whole. Feudalism was developing rapidly, and the major occupation of feudal lords seems to have been fighting. 'War among them was chronic. This warfare made commerce and other peaceful pursuits difficult, and produced a sag in morals.'[11] There were persistent attempts by the church to bring society closer to Christian values, and one of these was the enforcement of what was called 'The Peace of God'.

At the end of the tenth century in France, a project was begun which attempted to prevent attack on all places and people consecrated by the church (clergy, monks, virgins, churches, monasteries), and to stop fighting on Sundays. Later, exemption from attack was claimed for all those protected by the church, such as the poor, pilgrims, crusaders, and merchants on their journeys.

43

Another attempt to bring society closer to Christian standards began in the eleventh century. 'The Truce of God' forbade fighting from Saturday night to Monday morning, and on holy days of the church's year. Yet a further attempt by the church to curb war found expression a century later in the Second Lateran Council of 1139, barring jousts and tournaments in which private feuds were glorified by public blood-shedding.

During the eleventh century, the geographical expansion of the faith in Europe had gathered momentum, and the founding of the monastic orders was securing a deepening awareness of the meaning of the gospel, at least in these communities. At this time, however, religious expansion began to be associated with the expansion of Europe itself, and a new semi-Christian militarism emerged in the shape of the Crusades.

There were political and economic factors underlying the Crusades, as well as an extreme and misguided sort of religious devotion. It was the religious factors, however, at least on the surface, which were most important. One concern was the rescue of the holy places of Palestine, especially Jerusalem, from the Muslims, to bring them into Christian hands. Another was the protection of the Byzantine Empire against the aggresive Turks. Linked in with these were the concerns of the Popes to heal the breach between the western and eastern parts of the Catholic Church.

In 1096 Pope Urban II preached a strong sermon at Clermont in France, calling for troops to enlist against the Turks. 'God wills it', the congregation responded, and the 'First Crusade', as it has come to be known, was launched. Under the banner of the cross, many troops left for Asia Minor and eventually Jerusalem, where they indulged in much slaughter, pillage and destruction.

Several waves of Crusades followed during the next two hundred years. Here was a quasi-Christian militarism of a particularly ruthless sort. It was thought of as a 'holy war' fought for God (though not, we may recall, in the sense in which we used that term for the holy wars of the Old Testament, in which God fought for his people). The Crusading spirit was blessed and encouraged by the hierarchy of the church. Some military orders arose from the Crusades. Their members took vows of poverty, chastity and obedience, but their dedication was to the armies of Christ. The Knights Templars and Hospitallers are among the best known.

What is significant about the Crusades is that they were an attempt to further the kingdom of God on earth by military means. They were an attempt to use the means of the earthly city to build the City of God. Though there were some Christians who believed that the whole venture was at total odds with the New Testament gospel, most Christians of Western Europe accepted the Crusades: they went with the blessing of the Popes, and no Crusade was valid without papal endorsement.

What we see in the Crusades, therefore, is a complete reversal of the attitude of the early Christians towards war. In the early church, most Christians did not enlist in military service. Later the idea was developed that wars could be 'just'. Now some wars are regarded as 'holy'. 'They were an aspect of the partial capture of the church by the warrior tradition . . .'.[12]

Over these centuries, by far the most important theological discussion of war comes from the pen of Thomas Aquinas (1225–1274), although this only occupies a very minor part of his writings. Aquinas brought together the natural law tradition and biblical theology, and – building on the views of Augustine – refined Christian thinking on the 'just war'. In his *Summa Theologica* he writes:

> In order for a war to be just, three things are necessary. First the authority of the sovereign by whose command the war is to be waged.
>
> Secondly, a just cause is required, namely that those who are attacked, should be attacked because they deserve it on account of some fault . . .

Thirdly, it is necessary that the belligerents should have a rightful intention... [Here Aquinas quotes from Augustine: 'True religion looks upon as peaceful those wars that are waged not for motives of aggrandisement, or cruelty, but with the object of securing peace, of punishing evildoers, and of uplifting the good. ... Those who wage war justly aim at peace.'][13]

However, Aquinas argues, 'warlike pursuits are altogether incompatible with the duties of a bishop and a cleric', partly because they hinder the mind from divine things, and partly because, as ministers of the sacrament of the blood of Christ, it is unfitting for clerics to engage in war in which blood will be shed.

Here, then, we find both an awareness of the necessity for war in a sinful world, and its moral permissibility provided it be just, together with an acknowledgment also that there is a deep incongruence between shedding blood and the ministry of the gospel.

It was on the basis of this discussion in Aquinas that the Spanish theologian Francisco de Vitoria (1483–1546) developed a law of war. He argued against the king's treatment of the American Indians, and sought to define the limits of justice in going to war and in waging war. He offers a 'few canons or rules of warfare'. First, assuming that a prince has authority to make war, his first duty is to live if possible at peace with all men. He must remember that others are his neighbours, and that there can be no grounds for joy in 'killing and destroying men whom God has created and for whom Christ died'. Only 'under compulsion and reluctantly should he come to necessity of war'. Secondly, 'when war for a just cause has broken out, it must not be waged so as to ruin the people against whom it is directed', but only to secure one's rights and the defence of one's country so that peace and security will result. Thirdly, when victory is won and the war is over, the victory should be utilized 'with moderation and Christian humility'.

In his lengthy discussion of the rights of the Indians in the face of Spanish conquests in the New World, Vitoria affirmed the immunity of those who were not combatants in the fighting, arguing for the equal rights of both Spaniards and Indians. Non-combatant immunity became an important criterion in the theory of the just war, discussed by later writers in terms of 'discrimination' and 'proportion'. Vitoria also allowed for the rights of some conscientious objection.[14]

Another Spanish theologian, Francisco Suarez (1548–1617), discussed these same issues. He concludes that while war is not, absolutely speaking, intrinsically evil, nor forbidden to Christians, and that defensive war is not only permitted, but may even be commanded, nonetheless war must be 'justly waged'. In order for a war to be justly waged, a number of conditions have to be observed:

– the war must be waged by a legitimate power, such as the state or the sovereign prince;
– the cause itself and the reason for the war must be just;
– the method of the conduct of the war must be just, and 'due proportion' observed at its beginning, during its prosecution and after victory.

Many other Counter-Reformation theologians discussed these issues. The 'just war' thinking of Aquinas and these later Catholic theologians found its way into legal theory through the writings of Hugo Grotius. In 1625 this Dutch lawyer wrote *On the Law of War and Peace* in which he discusses the questions already explored by Vitoria and Suarez. Is war ever justified? What constitutes a just cause (*jus ad bellum*)? How is war to be conducted justly (*jus in bello*)? His rules for justice in war have been the basis for much modern international law.

The Reformation period and after

The period of the Reformation was a time of much civil unrest and international friction. The great theologians of the day gave themselves to discussion of the question whether or not it could be right for governments to wage war, and of the rights and wrongs of Christian participation in war. The primary issue which divided the Anabaptists from the other Reformation traditions was the relation of the church to the state. This is a question which will later occupy our attention; it underlies much of the present disagreement between Christian pacifist and Christian just-war theorists today. Both Luther and Calvin supported the state's use of force in war as a Christian duty at times. This was in contrast to the Mennonite Anabaptists who taught that Christians were called to total pacifism, basing this on a total separation of church and state.

Menno Simmons (1496–1561), from whom the Mennonites take their name, believed that the Scriptures teach that there are two opposing princes, and two opposing kingdoms: the one is the Prince of Peace, the other is the prince of strife. The Christian is a follower of the Prince of Peace, is commanded to love his enemies, to do good to those who persecute him, to turn the other cheek when struck.

> Tell me, how can a Christian defend scripturally retaliation, rebellion, war, striking, slaying, torturing, stealing, robbing and plundering and burning cities and conquering countries? . . . All rebellion is of the flesh and of the devil. . . .
>
> O blessed reader, our weapons are not swords and spears, but patience, silence and hope and the Word of God. . . .
>
> True Christians do not know vengeance, no matter how they are mistreated . . . they have beaten their swords into ploughshares and their spears into pruning hooks. . . . They think and desire and know nothing but peace; and are prepared to forsake country, goods, life and all for the sake of peace. . . .[15]

Here we find a total separation between the Christian community, to be marked by peace, and the earthly kingdoms of the prince of darkness.

Very different was the view of Martin Luther. His doctrine of the 'Two Kingdoms' led to a view of the state as a necessary institution of God with a divinely given task to restrain sin. As the state has to ward off the chaos which always threatens internally because of sin through the use of law, so externally it uses war to ward off the threat to peace and order posed by foreign enemies. According to the Lutheran theologian Helmut Thielicke[16], Luther sees a kind of logical connection between the existence of the state and the necessity of war. This may be seen at the very outset of his work on *Whether Soldiers, Too, Can Be Saved*, where he refers to his earlier work on *Temporal Authority* in which he made this connection, and then continues: 'For the very fact that the sword has been instituted by God to punish the evil, protect good, and preserve peace (Rom.13:1–4; 1 Pet.2:13–14), is powerful and sufficient proof that war and killing along with all the things that accompany wartime and martial law have been instituted by God. What else is war but the punishment of wrong and evil? Why does anyone go to war, except because he desires peace and obedience?'

Luther, in other words, regarded war as issuing from the political order as such. But there is another factor in his thought to which Thielicke refers: even the office of the sword can be an expression of love. Just as a good doctor may sometimes have to amputate in what, 'from the point of view of the organ', appears to be a cruel and merciless way, though from the point of view of the body is a saving action, so the soldier fulfilling his office even by killing the wicked, can be doing the work of love in protecting the good and promoting peace.

Thielicke then comments:

We would simply note here in passing the extraordinary simplification which marked Luther's age. In virtue of it he can conceive of war as an encounter between good and evil. Hence his analogy of the doctor versus the disease-ridden limbs, or law and order versus the criminals. The quotation once again helps us realise how very difficult it is to integrate the complex problems of modern world wars into the framework of police actions which Luther had in view. However simplified this conception of war, at least it shows clearly how Luther ascribes to the office of the sword – and to legal order – as controlling impulses love of neighbour and the desire to protect, help and save.[17]

There are issues here to which we shall return in Part 3.

As a final example from the Reformation period we turn to Calvin. Specifically against the pacifism of the Anabaptists, Calvin maintained both the right of the government to wage war, and also the urgency of restraint and humanity in the conduct of war. He leans heavily on Old Testament examples. He seems more firmly in the Augustinian tradition than Luther. Like Luther, he wishes to extrapolate from Paul's teaching in Romans 13 about the state as God's servant to restrain the evil-doer within, to justify the state's action in restraining the evil-doer without. He also operates with an understanding of war as a sort of extension of policing.

His reasons for this extrapolation are made clear in *Institutes*, where he writes first 'On the right of the government to wage war'. Kings and people must sometimes take up arms to execute public vengeance, and such wars may be judged lawful. 'For if power has been given them to preserve the tranquillity of their domain, to restrain the seditious stirrings of restless men, to help those forcibly oppressed, to punish evil deeds – can they use it more opportunely than to check the fury of one who disturbs both the repose of private individuals and the common tranquillity of all, who raises seditious tumults, and by whom violent oppression and vile misdeeds are perpetrated?' Calvin argues that both natural equity and the nature of the political office dictate that 'princes must be armed not only to restrain the misdeeds of private individuals by judicial punishment, but also to defend by war the dominions entrusted to their safekeeping if at any time they are under enemy attack.' And, in deliberate opposition to the Anabaptists, he writes: 'the Holy Spirit declares such wars to be lawful by many testimonies of Scripture' (though he does not say which).[18]

Leaning heavily on Augustine, Calvin then urges 'restraint and humanity in war':

> If anyone objects against me that in the New Testament there exists no testimony or example which teaches that war is a thing lawful for Christians, I answer first that the reason for waging war which existed of old still persists today; and that, on the other hand, there is no reason that bars magistrates from defending their subjects. Secondly, I say that an express declaration of this matter is not to be sought in the writings of the apostles; for their purpose is not to fashion a civil government but to establish the spiritual Kingdom of Christ.[19]

Finally, Calvin continues, basing his thinking on Luke 3:14:

> When he told them to be content with their wages, he certainly did not forbid them to bear arms. . . .
> But it is the duty of all magistrates here to guard particularly against giving vent to their passions even in the slightest degree. Rather, if they have to punish, let them not be carried away with headlong anger, or be seized with hatred, or burn with implacable severity. Let them also (as Augustine says) have pity on the common nature in the one whose special fault they are punishing. Or, if they must arm themselves against the enemy, that is the armed robber, let them not lightly seek occasion to do so; indeed, let them not accept the occasion when offered, unless they are driven to it by extreme necessity. For if we must perform much more than the heathen philosopher [referring to Cicero] required when he wanted war to seem a seeking of peace, surely everything else ought to be tried before recourse is had to arms. Lastly, in both situations let them not allow themselves to be swayed by any private affection,

but be led by concern for the people alone.[20]

Since these classic treatises of the Reformation period, Christian thinking has fallen mainly within the two strands of 'just war theory' and 'Christian pacifism'. The former, by way of Augustine and Aquinas, has been the teaching of the Catholic Church through to the Second Vatican Council of 1965. In the report from that Council on the Church in the Modern World, *Gaudium et Spes*, the wording is very restrained, however, and war is acknowledged only as a tragic necessity in some circumstances. 'It is one thing to wage a war of self-defence; it is quite another to seek to impose domination on another nation.' The Council, quite properly, is much more concerned with the devastatingly more horrendous questions raised by the 'total warfare' of modern weapons, to which we shall give our attention later.

Many Christians in the 'main line' denominations have followed the 'just war' tradition. One of the most eloquent recent advocates of this view, believing himself to be in line with Augustine and Aquinas, is the Protestant theologian Paul Ramsey. He explores how modern war could be conducted 'justly' in a world in which thermonuclear weapons are such an awful reality.[21]

The Christian pacifist tradition was a minority viewpoint led primarily by the sects. There was a firm reaction against the warlike Christianity of the Crusades by the Waldenses, and we have quoted the writings of the founder of the Mennonites at the time of the Reformation. The Quaker movement, following George Fox (1624–91), is also identified with opposition to war. Fox said, 'I live in virtue of that life and power that takes away the vocation of all wars.'[22] And Robert Barclay (1648–90) wrote: 'It is not lawful for Christians to resist evil or to fight in any cause. . . . [War is] as opposite to the Spirit and doctrine of Christ as light to darkness.'[23]

There was no upsurge of Christian pacifism on any large scale, however, until after World War I. More recently the influence of the Mennonite tradition, together with the establishment of many groups like the Anglican Pacifist Fellowship, Christian CND, Christians For Peace, and so on, indicate a much wider pacifist influence in the church. Some Christians are pacifist in the older sense of a complete rejection of any war as incompatible with the gospel of Christ. One of the clearest theological statements is that of G. H. C. Macgregor, *The New Testament Basis of Pacifism*[24]. One of the most eloquent recent writings is R. Sider's *Nuclear Holocaust and Christian Hope*[25].

Increasing numbers of Christians are turning to what has (perhaps misleadingly) become called 'nuclear pacifism'. Many 'nuclear pacifists' may well embrace a 'just war' type of theological position, but on that basis believe that neither the use nor even the possession of nuclear weapons can be justified. These are questions to which we shall return in Part 4.

Both 'just war' and 'Christian pacifist' strands have been forced into a radical rethinking in recent years. Pacifists have had to ask: Can such evils as Nazism be met with other than a coercive use of force? Just warriors have been forced to consider: Given the awful possibilities of modern warfare, can one be anything other than pacifist? Theology is not and cannot be unaffected by the scale and devastation of two world wars this century. The whole theological as well as political agenda has had to be rethought in a new light since Hiroshima. We will look at the fresh reappraisal which this century's experience requires of the Christian community in Chapter 5.

But, we may wonder, why have Christians spoken with so many different voices? Why is there no united view? It appears that it is not only their political contexts that are so diverse. We find different ways of using the Bible in ethical decision-making; we find different views of the Christian's relationship to the state in the purposes of God. We find, in fact, different *theological* approaches to the questions. It is at the level of the theological understanding of the world and the Christian's role within it that our thinking needs to begin.

Before we come to that task ourselves, however, let us summarize our journey so far.

Notes for chapter three

[1]J. M. Hornus, *It is not Lawful for me to Fight*, rev. ed. tr. A. Kreider & O. Coburn (Herald Press & Paternoster, 1980), p.90.

[2]K. S. Latourette, *A History of Christianity* (Eyre & Spottiswoode, 1954), p.243.

[3]Tertullian, *On Idolatry*, 19. *cf.* R. E. O. White's discussion in *The Changing Continuity of Christian Ethics*, 2 (Paternoster, 1981), p.69ff.

[4]Origen, *Contra Celsum*, esp. III.7 and V.33.

[5]Lactantius, *The Divine Institutes*, VI.20:15–17.

[6]Ambrose, *On the Christian Faith*, 2.16.

[7]Ambrose, *de officiis* i.35.

[8]Augustine, 'Letter to Count Boniface', letter 189, in A. Holmes' *War and Christian Ethics* (Baker, 1978), p.61.

[9]*Cf.* R. E. O. White, *The Changing Continuity of Christian Ethics*, 2 (Paternoster, 1981), p.111.

[10]In *Ibid.*, p.112.

[11]K. S. Latourette, *op.cit.*, p.365.

[12]*Ibid.*, p.414.

[13]Aquinas, *Summa Theologica* 2.2, Q.40.

[14]*Cf.* A. Holmes, *War and Christian Ethics* (Baker, 1978), p.118ff.

[15]Menno Simmons, quoted in A. Holmes *op.cit.*, p.186.

[16]H. Thielicke, *Theological Ethics*, 2 (English Translation, Eerdmans, 1969), p.423.

[17]*Ibid.*, p.424.

[18]J. Calvin, *Institutes*, IV.xx.11–12.

[19]*Ibid.*

[20]*Ibid.*

[21]P. Ramsey, *War and the Christian Conscience* (Duke University Press, 1961).

[22]G. Fox in R. H. Bainton, *Christian Attitudes to War and Peace* (Hodder, 1961), p.157f.

[23]R. Barclay, *Apology* XV.ii.

[24]G. H. C. Macgregor, *The New Testament Basis of Pacifism*, 2nd ed. (Fellowship of Reconciliation, 1953).

[25]Hodder & Stoughton, 1983.

4 'Just warriors' or Christian pacifists?

It is now time to take stock, and offer a summary of the two main ways in which Christians have approached the ethics of war and the rights and wrongs of military service. We will look back first over the just war tradition which draws on the thinking of Ambrose, Augustine, Aquinas, Luther, Calvin, and the Catholic tradition. Then we will summarize the Christian pacifist traditions, given expression in the early Fathers, then the Waldenses, the Mennonites and Quakers. Both are live options for many Christian thinkers today.

The 'just war' tradition

We can summarize the main points of the 'just war' doctrine in these terms:

(i) The tradition does not offer a justification for war as such; war is never thought of as other than an evil, although sometimes it is justified as a lesser evil. We must distinguish carefully between the crusader mentality and just war theory. There is no place for a crusading militarism in most of the just war tradition. The professed aim of 'just warriors' is peace through the vindication of justice.

(ii) There are circumstances in which it is morally permissible for the proper authority of the state to have recourse to armed force, in legitimate defence of its people against aggression and the protection of dependants from being unjustly oppressed.

(iii) The 'just war' doctrine recognizes that in this as yet sin-affected world there will be wars and rumours of wars. It seeks to specify in which circumstances it could be just to engage in war. It also seeks to place limits on the way in which war is waged so that it is conducted justly.

(iv) The war may only be waged by the legitimate authority (of the 'prince' (Luther), or the 'magistrate' (Calvin)) of the state; there must be a formal declaration of war.

(v) The cause of the war must be just. (By 'cause' here is meant the 'final' cause, *i.e.* purpose for which the war is engaged; the triggering event is the *in*justice to which war is a response.)

(vi) The recourse to war must be the very last resort.

(vii) The motive of the war must be just.

(viii) There must be reasonable hope of success.

(ix) The good benefit to be expected from going to war

55

must outweigh the evils incurred in waging it.

(x) The criterion of discrimination: violence must only be directed to those in arms. The immunity of non-combatants must be preserved to the extent that no action may be taken deliberately to harm non-combatants. It is recognized, however, that there will inevitably be some harm caused to non-combatants through proximity to the activities of war, but this must be minimized, and as far as possible the enemy society and institutions must be protected. Non-combatant immunity is extended to cover humane treatment and care for enemy wounded and prisoners.

(xi) The criterion of proportion: the war must be waged in such a way that only the minimum of force needed to achieve the aims of the war may be used. The war must be conducted so that harm does not result which is disproportionate to the cause for which the war is waged.

It is obvious at once that many of these criteria would have been much more relevant to the more personalized wars of the Middle Ages than they could be to the possibilities of total war today. Some of the criteria do, however, underlie some of the international conventions of war, and in particular the criteria of discrimination and proportion are the basis of some rulings on military procedures. Furthermore, many of these criteria can, without too much alteration, be seen to have relevance for conventional modern warfare, such as the conflict between Britain and Argentina over the Falkland Islands in 1982. They underlie also much of the discussion in, for example, the theology of liberation, about the rights and wrongs of a 'just revolution'.

On what Christian principles has the just war doctrine been based? There seem to be six main theological emphases:

(i) God is a just God who cares about justice. It is a Christian obligation to work for justice especially for the poor and the oppressed, and to vindicate justice by opposing injustice, if necessary by force.

(ii) The sinful nature of man and the fallenness of our social order mean that men and societies do sometimes act unjustly towards fellow human beings. There is an aggressive and acquisitive side to human nature which needs to be held in check.

(iii) God has ordained the authorities of the state to uphold goodness and justice and to punish evil. It is part of the God-given function of the state to use such force as may be necessary to carry out its divinely appointed task.

(iv) The preservation of 'peace' at the expense of justice is against the will of God. Sadly, sometimes, Christians have to fight for the peace which is the consequence of justice. 'Peace at any price' is no peace at all.

(v) At all times, the state must hold to the priority of human values and the dignity of all men before God. War can only be waged as a lesser evil, in such a way that the 'spirit of the peacemaker' is preserved, and the humane treatment of non-combatants and enemy prisoners is ensured as they are made in the image of God.

(vi) The cross of Christ displays the willingness of God to wage war on the powers of evil, to the point of self-sacrifice. At the cross of Christ, God 'disarmed the principalities and powers and made a public example of them, triumphing over them in him' (Col.2:15). The Christian is called to follow Christ in standing firmly for the cause of righteousness, and the state is the 'servant of God to execute his wrath on the wrongdoer' (Rom.13:4).

The pacifist tradition

The main theme of the Christian pacifist tradition can be stated more briefly. As the heading of one of the leaflets of the Anglican Pacifist Fellowship puts it: 'Christianity is a Pacifist Faith'. The Christian pacifist approach depends on the fundamental convictions outlined by G. H. C. Macgregor in his influential book *The New Testament Basis of Pacifism*[1]: first, Jesus' ethic is centred on love towards one's neighbour; secondly, this ethic is in turn based on the belief in a Father God who loves all men impartially and sets an infinite (*sic*) value on every individual human soul; thirdly, all the teaching of Jesus must be interpreted in the light of his own way of life, and above all of the cross by which his teaching was sealed.

Macgregor then says:

> The issue before us is therefore best framed not by asking, 'Does the New Testament ethic ever allow the use of force in the resisting and conquering of evil?' So to pose the question is to invite that unfortunate confusion of 'pacifism' with 'passivism'. We shall rather ask, 'What is the specifically Christian way of meeting and overcoming evil, as set forth in the teaching, example and cross of Jesus Christ? Can war under any circumstances be held to be consistent with that way?'[2]

He goes on to argue that there is a distinction between moral and immoral uses of force, and that although some limited exercise of force may well fall within the New Testament ethic, war so stultifies the specifically Christian method of meeting evil that its one certain issue will not be justice but moral and spiritual death. Whatever may be said of certain exercises of force, war at least – it is clear to the pacifist – must be under a final prohibition.

Much Christian pacifist writing turns first to the Sermon on the Mount:

> 'Blessed are the peacemakers, for they shall be called sons of God . . . You have heard that it was said, "An eye for an eye and a tooth for a tooth." But I say to you, Do not resist one who is evil. But if any one strikes you on the right cheek, turn to him the other also; . . . You have heard that it was said, "You shall love your neighbour and hate your enemy." But I say to you, Love your enemies and pray for those who persecute you' (Mt.5:9,38–39, 43–44).

This teaching is then interpreted to apply to both private and public morality, within a theoretical framework which usually includes these themes:

(i) Jesus made no distinction between private morality and public morality. He never suggested a double standard for his followers as individuals on the one hand and as members of a community on the other. His teaching is meant to be obeyed in both individual and community life.

(ii) The Old Testament, to which recourse is often made in attempts to justify the necessity for war, in fact points to the way God worked by miracle (at the Exodus, and with Gideon, for example) through his people's vulnerability. Their trust was not in chariots, but in the power of God to defend them.

(iii) In the incarnation of Jesus we see the God of all power becoming defenceless. Jesus' example of non-retaliation against evil is the Christian way.

(iv) The state's role is to maintain law and order within society; the law-breaker may be resisted and restrained in order that justice may be done. In international relations, however, the question is not that of disciplining the 'law-breaker'; it is illegitimate to argue from Romans 13, for example, about questions of international warfare.

(v) The Christian way is to witness to the power of the gospel and the message of love, by actually putting into practice the teaching of Christ. The church is to 'overcome evil with good'. What is lacking, it seems, is faith in the power of Christ and his gospel to overcome conflict and to reconcile enemies.

(vi) Christ calls for unqualified obedience despite all risks. We cannot 'love our enemy' by killing him. We are called as a Christian community to work for reconciliation. If only all Christians took their commitment to Christ seriously enough to renounce the way of violence, then the world would understand that Christianity is a pacifist faith. 'Only in this way will it be possible for Christianity to become what Jesus promised it would be, an irresistible force in the world.'[3]

(vii) The way of the cross is the way of self-giving love and of passive, non-violent resistance to violence. Jesus' triumph over evil was precisely through his refusal to retaliate, and his demonstration of God's love of the unjust to the point of self-sacrifice. We are called to be 'sheep amongst wolves'.

(viii) Pacifism is not simply a Christian witness to an alternative way, although it is that. It would also be practical politics if it was tried. The real alternative to war – active pacifism – has never yet been tried. There is no question of yielding to tyranny: it is rather a question of by what method it is to be resisted. Jesus and the early Christians stood fast to their principles, but they rejected the way of violence.

We have spoken of the 'tradition' of pacifism, but we should not forget that there is a spectrum of emphases under the pacifist umbrella. There is an *absolutist pacifism* such as we find in the writings of Leo Tolstoy. In one of his last books, *The Law of Love and the Law of Violence*, he rejects all institutional forms of Christianity, together with all the violence he believes is implicit in the institutions of the state – and all the violence of revolutionaries who aim to overthrow it. The whole currency of aggression in all its forms is profitless compared with the law of love. Pacifism belongs with anarchism. Total pacifism implies no institutional constraint over the lives of others at all. At the other end of the pacifist spectrum there is the *pragmatic pacifism* of those who believe that it is simply the best way forward for human societies and human individuals to walk the pacifist path. Between these two extremes come pacifists like Macgregor, who sees the necessity for some institutional constraints against evil, but the violence of war as morally prohibited.

A simple polarity will not do

It is too simplistic to set up the debate in terms of *either* justice *or* peace, although some Christians have tended to do so. It is not the case that 'just warriors' are concerned only for justice and that it is the pacifists who are the peacemakers. The issues are much more complex, and the theological relationship between justice and peace much more profound.

Because of this complexity, however, which will occupy us

later, we can begin to see that the debate is not always as sharply polarized as it has sometimes been presented. Both traditions seek to make peace. And both (apart from absolute pacifists) acknowledge the need for civil order and some use of force. The issues of disagreement seem to come down primarily to three, and we can express them as different ways of holding complex issues in tension.

The first line of tension to be drawn concerns the nature of human life. We have to take seriously being 'in Adam' as well as 'in Christ'. The question is, where do we mark the point between human trustworthiness and untrustworthiness? Is our nature such that the violence within requires some ordering restraint and deterrence? Christians of the just war tradition often claim that pacifists have too optimistic a view of human nature, that they try to live as though the kingdom of God had already fully come, and as though violent sinful passions were no longer operative. Christians of the just war tradition would say that they, too, long for peace, but that because of human sin and untrustworthiness, the way to peace can only be found through justice and the coercive use of force in the face of evil.

Christians of the pacifist traditions, on the other hand, tend to see Christians who hold the just war theory as failing to take the gospel seriously enough. The kingdom of God has come into this world in Jesus, and though not in its fulness yet, it is present reality, and needs to be manifested in the lives of Christ's disciples. God's spiritual resources *are* available to Christian people who are called on, whatever the odds, to live out their new life, going beyond the demands of justice. It is not that justice is the way to peace; the pacifist would rather say: peace is the way.

Here, then, is the first issue for our theological agenda. How do we view human nature? In the world of real politics, it is possible to live the life of the kingdom of God?

The second area of tension concerns the place of the state in God's purposes for the world, and a Christian's relationship to the 'powers that be'. At one end of this tension is the view that the state is a God-given institution to be obeyed. It exists for God to maintain order and justice in this world, and Christians must be committed to its legitimate and God-given authority. At the other end of this line is the view that the state is given as a concession to human sin, and although God uses the pagan state as an instrument in his purposes – as he used the pagan Cyrus as his servant – the Christian is not to be part of such a society. Christians are instead called to witness to an alternative way of living; to be in the world, but not 'of' it. So here is another theological question: what is a Christian's relationship to the state?

Thirdly, there is a line to be drawn between different uses of force, and the question here is the point at which limits have to be set to the use of force. Many pacifists believe that some coercive force (like family discipline and civil police force) is essential, but that to resort to the violence of warfare is to cross a moral boundary. The state, they say, may not kill. The just war theory, however, allows the state sometimes to kill, but only in the cause of justice and not in an indiscriminate and disproportionate way. Where is the cut-off point in the use of force?

These are some of the concerns we will have to explore further in Part 3. At this point, let us briefly examine some of the problems of applying 'just war' and 'pacifist' thinking to the modern world.

In recent days it would be difficult to point to many modern wars and say unambiguously, 'That was a just war' within the terms of the tradition. Now of course it is no part of the just war theory that wars are *in fact* fought justly, but only that they *should* be (as it is no part of Christian thinking that Christians do not in fact sin, although they should not). Therefore the fact that there are few historical examples of just wars does not necessarily count against the just war theory. However, a war which may begin with an apparently just cause seems inevitably to change its intention and rationale as the war proceeds, so that the question needs to be asked whether it is actually possible to wage war justly in the modern world, or whether injustice is endemic to modern warfare.

Many Christians, for example, believed that World War II started with a just cause. A strong case could be made for the justice of combatting the evil aggression of Hitler. Indeed, a case was made for the Christian duty of engaging in war against Nazism. However, by 1944 it was the almost lone voice of Bishop Bell of Chichester in the House of Lords which challenged the government's policy of obliteration bombing of Hamburg and Berlin. 'That is not a justifiable act of war,' he declared.[4] 'To justify methods inhumane in themselves by arguments of expediency smacks of the Nazi philosophy that "Might is Right".' Bishop Bell urged a much more careful discrimination between military and non-military objectives, believing that on the criteria of the 'just war', obliteration bombing was utterly indiscriminate and disproportionate, and therefore morally unacceptable.

Viscount Cranborne's reply was revealing. He acknowledged that 'the great centres of administration, of production and of communication are themselves military targets in a total war', and he argued that to hinder enemy action by bringing 'the whole life of cities to a standstill' was a 'full justification' for the policy of obliteration bombing. Did he mean that the traditional discrimination between combatants and non-combatants becomes an impossible distinction in a 'total war' between modern states, and that industrial and administrative centres are equally 'military targets'? If that is so, we need to ask whether the traditional 'just war' distinctions can in fact hold in an age of modern 'total war', or whether, with Bishop Bell, we must insist that the *only* justifiable actions in modern war are those in which distinctions between combatants and non-combatants can be realistically maintained. Either way the question 'Was World War II just?' has no easy answer.

Even in 1944, the mushroom cloud over Hiroshima was still in the unknown future, and the growing, complex interaction of military, industrial, technological and diplomatic factors which have been a feature of the post-war arms race was only beginning. Can 'just war' thinking have any relevance to the nuclear age? Can nuclear war be waged 'justly'? Can the values which the just war theory was established to maintain – namely a society with justice as the basis for securing human life and welfare – actually be defended by modern war? Here are some of the modern problems to which Christian 'just warriors' need to give attention.

Today's Christian pacifist has problems as well. He will want to take with utmost seriousness the word of Christ: 'Blessed are the peacemakers'. He may, though, have a nagging feeling that while an individual Christian may be called to a pacifist viewpoint, this is not something which he can urge on the community as a whole. Is it not, after all, part of the rationale of the state that its citizens and those who expect its protection – particularly the young and the infirm – shall be defended if their safety is threatened? Perhaps being a pacifist could be right for individual conscientious objectors, but is it really a Christian calling to urge the nation as a whole to martyrdom? And that of course is what pacifism in the face of modern warfare might lead to. Macgregor points out the risk:

A nation, following the way of Christ, might feel called upon to adopt a policy of total disarmament. But it would do so, in the first instance, not with the deliberate purpose of courting martyrdom, but with the conviction that the best safety from the perils against which nations arm is to be found in a new national way of life, which would remove causes of provocation and lead progressively to reconciliation and peace. It, too, would risk everything on the conviction that God's way would work. But such a nation must also be willing, if necessary, to incur the risk of national martyrdom by refusing to equip itself against the possibility of aggression. And it may be that the world must wait for its redemption from warfare until one nation is ready to risk crucifixion at the hands of its possible enemies. It might lose its own national life; but it would set free such a flood of spiritual life as would save the world. To many of us this may not be a very welcome or comforting implication to discover in the Cross.[5]

What Macgregor does not face squarely enough is that his position may require him to *call* his nation to self-destruction in the face of evil.

But, we may properly reply, while it may be a Christian calling to risk martyrdom for oneself, on what grounds may a Christian commend to his government that they risk martyrdom for other people or indeed call them to do so? It is not only the loss of national identity, or national honour, that is at stake when considering armed aggression from an enemy in the modern world. It is loss of life, of cultural traditions, of buildings and works of art, of habitable earth, of ecological balance, of the possible future health of generations yet to be born, and so on. Can a Christian ask his government to risk that in the light of the command of God to be a steward of his world? Not many pacifists would go all the way with the absolutists, in rejecting *any* coercive use of force (which would of course mean no police, no punishment, no prison, no school or family discipline). That would mean, in effect, the total breakdown of all order. Most would argue for a right and a wrong use of force, and that it is the wrong use of force in war that they condemn. But this is to beg the question. Is it a right use of force to resist, and if necessary to kill, an armed intruder who is attacking your daughter? Is it a right use of force to storm an embassy in which innocent civilians are being held hostage at gunpoint by terrorists, and being killed one by one at intervals? Is it a right use of force to resist the armed invasion of unprotected Falkland Islanders? Some who are pacifists by personal conviction reluctantly concede that in the modern world of technologically powered evil, the quest for the way of Christ sometimes involves fighting for justice.

We are beginning to see that there is no easy line. A simple polarity between justice and peace therefore will not do. Our theological agenda needs to explore more deeply the relationship between them.

Notes for chapter four

[1] G. H. C. Macgregor, *The New Testament Basis of Pacifism*, 2nd ed. (Fellowship of Reconciliation, 1953), p.11f.
[2] *Ibid.*, p.12.
[3] G. Wilson, *Christianity is a Pacifist Faith* (Anglican Pacifist Fellowship) undated pamphlet.
[4] Hansard, Wednesday 9 February 1944, **130**, col.741.
[5] G. H. C. Macgregor, *op.cit.*, p.74f.

5 Frightened new world

We are now able to see that there is no easy progression from the biblical examples to today's questions. Nor is there any uniformly agreed teaching from the traditions of the Christian church. This does not, however, mean that we have to start from scratch, and that neither the Bible nor the traditions are any help at all. On the contrary, they remind us that our questions need to be asked – and perhaps even the questions themselves modified – within a theological context. We are going to have to start with our understanding of God, and the place of mankind and society within God's world. In other words, we need a *theology* of order and justice and peace to guide our thinking before we can make sense of how to work towards order and justice and peace in this confused world. When that context is clearer, then we shall be better able to make sense of the variety of biblical examples, then we shall be better equipped to make our own judgment about the views of other Christians in the past. This theological agenda will be our task in Part 3.

There is another reason also why we need a broad theological base from which to begin. Part of our problem is that many of today's questions are new ones, and do not easily fit within earlier Christian answers. The nature of modern warfare and the style of international power politics are transposing many of the old questions into a different key, and frequently posing new questions altogether. The situations in which the traditional Christian ethics of war were developed no longer exist. No more can we think, like Luther, of simple right and wrong, and of war simply as an extension of policing. We need a broader perspective altogether. Before we set out to formulate our theological foundation, therefore, we need to think further about the questions posed for us by our 'frightened new world'.

'A completely fresh reappraisal'

In the section 'Avoidance of War' in the Vatican II document *Gaudium et Spes*, the Council noted that 'as long as the danger of war persists, and there is no international authority with the necessary competence and power, governments cannot be denied the right of lawful self-defence, once all peace efforts have failed. ... However,' they continue, 'it is one thing to wage a war of self-defence, it is quite another to seek to impose domination on another nation.' They go on:

> The development of armaments by modern science has immeasurably magnified the horrors and wickedness of war. Warfare conducted by these weapons can inflict immense and indiscriminate havoc which goes far beyond the bounds of legitimate defence. ... All these factors force us to undertake a completely fresh reappraisal of war. Men of this generation should realise that they will have to render an account of their warlike behaviour; the destiny of generations to come depends largely on the decisions they make today.[1]

The Council further declared that 'Every act of war directed to the indiscriminate destruction of whole cities or vast areas with their inhabitants is a crime against God and man, which merits unequivocal condemnation. ... The arms race is one of the greatest curses on the human race and the harm

67

it inflicts on the poor is more than can be endured.'

That was in 1965.

World War II, with its saturation bombing of cities like Dresden and Coventry, and with the deaths of upwards of 70,000 people at Hiroshima and 40,000 at Nagasaki in August 1945, each from one bomb from one aircraft, has opened a new age of 'total warfare'. The bombs which fell on Berlin, condemned by Bishop Bell in the House of Lords, were indiscriminate in effect. 'Little Boy', the euphemistic name given to the bomb which destroyed Hiroshima, was indiscriminate by *design*. Although there have been recent moves towards accuracy in the counterforce tactics of 'theatre' nuclear weaponry (designed to attack specific military targets), *strategic* nuclear weapons and chemical and biological weapons are *designed* to be used in an indiscriminate and disproportionate way. Such modern weapons fail to recognize the distinctions to which Bishop Bell courageously but vainly appealed, between combatants and non-combatants (which made 'non-combatant immunity' a feasible goal, and hurt to civilians a tragic consequence rather than a deliberate necessity).

The scale and style of war has irrevocably altered. Whereas wars in the Middle Ages were largely personal in character, modern warfare has become utterly impersonal – a matter of military hardware and computer technology. Whereas in the Middle Ages it was possible for whole areas of society to escape any sense of direct involvement in war, and it was possible to think of war as something engaged in by the military, now, and indeed to some degree ever since the Napoleonic wars, everyone is in some sense a 'military person' – everyone is certainly part of the suffering which total war demands. Modern war requires that there can no longer be an uncommitted spectator. Furthermore, in a strategic nuclear exchange, even the distinction between the home front and the battle front has gone. (With increasingly accurate 'tactical' counterforce weapons, that line is beginning to be drawn again, but the unknown factor of likely radiation damage is no respecter of battle lines, and the critical problem of escalation makes this a very uncertain basis for argument.)

The devastating effects of nuclear warfare are almost too overwhelming to contemplate. At Hiroshima, the Little Boy bomb was 'only' a 13 kiloton yield, whereas a Polaris missile has a yield of about 660 kt and Cruise missiles, 200 kt. As the world knows, however, at Hiroshima it was the fortunate minority who were killed instantly. About 70,000 had died within the first month. By 1950 the death toll was nearer 200,000 (compared with 290,000 American direct battle casualties in the whole of World War II). Some died from burns, others from cancers, leukemia, delayed effects both physical and psychological. Some are still dying with genetic and radiation effects today. There is the continuing plight of those psychologically scarred: the reluctance of employers to take 'hibakusha' ('explosion-afflicted person'); the difficulty of finding a non-'hibakusha' spouse through fear of disease and genetic malformation; the rejection by the community making the hibakusha feel outcast. And quite apart from the personal suffering there is the as yet incalculable long-term radiation effect on the environment.

Medical services are not equipped to cope with suffering on such a total scale, as the report *The Medical Consequences of Nuclear Weapons*[2] makes clear. In the 1980 'Square Leg' NATO exercise there was an 'attack' on London using five nuclear weapons. Based on the 1971 census, when the population of Greater London was 7.2 million, blast effects alone would have resulted in 1.1 million immediate deaths, and 2.4 to 2.9 million injured. Only about 24,000 of the present 60,000 hospital beds would remain, of which about 15,000 would be equipped to handle casualties. Clearly not many of the 2.5 million or so injured and 250,000 burned could receive hospital treatment. Assuming doctors to be evenly distributed within the population at the time of the attack, about 4,000 to 6,000 of the original 11,500 would be expected to survive. If all the casualties could be brought to them

69

and they were prepared to work regardless of radiation risks for eighteen hours a day seeing each patient for twenty minutes, it would take between seven and seventeen days for all the injured to be examined and receive whatever treatment was available.

The doctor authors of the report conclude: 'An examination of the facts leads to one inescapable conclusion. If for none other than purely medical reasons, *nuclear warfare must never be allowed to happen*; it is not an option that can be contemplated by any government, however dire the consequences.'[3]

The more recent report of the British Medical Association's Board of Science and Education, *The Medical Effects of Nuclear War*, concludes in this way:

> The explosion of a single nuclear bomb of the size used at Hiroshima over a major city in the UK is likely to produce so many cases of trauma and burns requiring hospital treatment that the remaining medical services in the UK would be completely overwhelmed. An attack with, for example, 200 megatons, represents an explosive power some 15,000 times greater than the Hiroshima bomb; or the equivalent of forty times all the conventional explosives used in the whole of the second world war.
>
> The NHS could not deal with the casualties that might be expected following the detonation of a single one-megaton weapon over the UK. It follows that multiple nuclear explosions over several, possibly many, cities would force a breakdown in medical services across the country as a whole . . . we believe that such a weight of attack would cause the medical services in the country to collapse. The provision of individual medical or nursing attention for victims of a nuclear attack would become remote. At some point it would disappear completely and only the most primitive first aid services might be available from a fellow survivor.[4]

We have reached, then, what Helmut Thielicke calls a 'qualitatively different' stage with the advent of nuclear (that is, strategic nuclear, biological and chemical) weapons. 'The nuclear age confronts us,' he says, 'with a change not merely in the form, but in the very nature of war.'[5] For if the use of indiscriminate weapons of mass destruction is met by the same response by an enemy, then the *use* of such weapons is not merely an attack, it is also tantamount to suicide. And if an action undertaken in *defence* of a society leads in fact (in all probability) to the *annihilation* of that society, then we have reached a *reductio ad absurdum*. Thielicke writes:

> The state is an order of divine preservation in the fallen world. In prenuclear epochs war could still be regarded as an emergency instrument of this order. But in the atomic age war has ceased to serve any of the purposes of preservation and has become an exclusively destructive process. If what is to be defended is itself threatened by the act of defence, then the concept of a just war becomes highly dubious, if not completely invalid. Then the previously assumed connection between the state and war is broken in the sense that in principle, war is no longer a possibility within but a threat to the order of preservation.[6]

In other words, the concept of a just war as a war of *defence* remains meaningful only so long as defence is possible. But if we are talking of mutual annihilation, then the whole concept of a just war loses its meaning. Our theology needs to be written on a broader base, because of this 'completely fresh reappraisal' of war in the modern world.

Shifts in 'defence strategy' to 'deterrence'

Since World War II there has, of course, been a very significant shift in the West's military thinking. No longer is the chief purpose of the military establishment to wage wars and to be able to win them. The chief purpose of the military is now to avert them. So were born the various theories of nuclear deterrence, developing in the 1950s and 1960s, on which NATO philosophy has since been based. As Sir Neil Cameron wrote: 'The establishment of deterrence as the central basis of our defence policy has overturned a great deal of our defence thinking.'[7]

It is claimed that war has been averted for nearly forty years on the basis of deterrence – and that is mostly true of wars fought over Europe. There have, however, been many wars elsewhere since World War II, and it is a sobering political question to ask to what extent the 'wars' between the superpowers have been fought out in the Third World. How many European and American lives are being preserved at the cost of lives of people in Africa, South and Central America, the Middle East or South East Asia? (This argument is rejected, however, by the Institute for European Defence and Strategic Studies, as expounded in *Protest and Perish*[8].)

It is important to sketch out the way in which military thinking has altered. We can only offer a highly selective sketch of some significant events and statements, but they will, I think, indicate the main emphases on which we as Christians have to form a judgment.[9]

Following World War II, when only America had an atomic weapon, there were some attempts to bring all means of production of such weapons under international control. The first resolution of the first General Assembly of the United Nations in January 1946 was to set up a commission charged to bring proposals 'for the elimination from national armaments of atomic weapons'. The 'Baruch Plan' attempted to build in to the proposals factors that were more favourable to the United States than to Russia, in such a way that the latter's suspicions were raised and their veto was exercised. However, the Soviet delegate Andrei Gromyko countered with a proposal to destroy all weapons in existence and to cease all production. The US replied with the world's fourth nuclear explosion, a test over Bikini Atoll on 1 July 1946. In the view of the authors of *Defended to Death*, 'Bikini may have been called a test, but in truth it blew up one of the only two serious opportunities to bring nuclear weapons under international control.'

In 1949 the USSR, which had started research on its own nuclear weapons in 1942, exploded its own first bomb. The Cold War was well on its way.

During the 1950s, theories of nuclear deterrence were being aired. Now that 'both sides' had a nuclear capability, peace was to be kept through the development of a balance of terror. Churchill expressed it like this:

> A curious paradox has emerged. Let me put it simply. After a certain point has been passed, it may be said 'The worse things get, the better'. The broad effect of the latest developments [the H-bomb] is to spread almost indefinitely and at least to a vast extent the area of mortal danger. . . . Then it may well be that we shall by a process of sublime irony have reached a stage in this story where safety will be the sturdy child of terror, and survival the twin brother of annihilation.[10]

There was, however, a growing hope of a new diplomacy. Khrushchev's speech to the 20th Party Congress in February 1956 struck a new note: the principle of peaceful co-existence. 'In present day conditions, there is no other way out. Indeed, there are only two ways: either peaceful co-existence or the most destructive war in history. There is no third way.' But a number of factors soon changed the tone again. Suez was one. The Russian technological success with Sputnik was another. Now that the USSR had such a capability in space, the capacity for American deterrence could be called in question. Thirdly, the Cuban crisis in 1962 brought home very vividly the proximity and danger of nuclear war.

American Defense Secretary Robert McNamara was a key figure in the defence thinking of the early 1960s. Here are two significant quotations from what he has subsequently said.

In 1967 he referred back to the time when he was Secretary

of Defense in 1961, when 'the Soviet Union possessed a very small operational arsenal of intercontinental missiles'. The US administration sought to hedge against a theoretically possible Soviet build-up – the Russians had the capability, but there was no certainty that they actually intended to increase their arsenal substantially. 'Thus in the course of hedging against what was then only a theoretically possible Soviet build-up, we took decisions which have resulted in our current superiority in numbers of warheads and deliverable megatons. But the blunt fact remains that if we had had more accurate information about planned Soviet strategic forces, we simply would not have needed to build as large a nuclear arsenal as we have today.'[11]

Then again, referring in 1982 to a classified memorandum from himself to President Kennedy written in 1962 and subsequently made public, he quoted: '"It has become clear to me that the Air Force proposals are based on the objective of achieving a first-strike capability. . . . I reaffirm now my belief that the full first-strike capability . . . should be rejected as a US policy option."' That was in 1962. In 1982 he said: 'Read again my memo to President Kennedy. It scares me today to read the damn thing. What that means is the Air Force supported the development of US forces sufficiently large to destroy so much of the Soviet nuclear force, by a first strike, that there would not be enough left to cause us any concern if they shot at us. My God! If the Soviets thought that was our objective, how would you expect them to react? The way they reacted was by substantially expanding their strategic nuclear weapons programme. . . .'

Hence the beginnings of the huge build-up of forces on 'both sides'.

Flexible response

During the 1960s the balance of terror was maintained by commitment to a policy of Mutual Assured Destruction – by having sufficient capability to scare the other side from making a first strike because of the availability of resources for massive retaliation. However, the Americans had another question to face: how to keep their NATO commitment to Europe. The strategic intercontinental missiles might keep a balance of terror between the superpowers. But how was America to react if there was a Soviet aggressive move against Europe? So was born the idea of 'flexible response'. Whatever the Soviets decided to do, the West needed to be able to match it with something at a similar or slightly more devastating level. The thinking was that a Western ability to respond at every level – from conventional to small nuclear attack, with the eventual possibility of an all-out strategic nuclear strike – left open the risk of nuclear war sufficiently for the Soviets not to know how the West would respond. Because of this doubt about the level of the West's response, the Soviets would, it was argued, be deterred from any first strike.

There were two serious consequences of the NATO doctrine of flexible response. One was the cost. To maintain a many-levelled nuclear capability was very expensive – much more than the cost simply of basing one's defence on strategic missiles alone. Secondly, the threshold between nuclear and conventional weapons became blurred. What we have now is a whole range of nuclear weapons, some strategic (intercontinental), some 'tactical' (which can be thought of as more limited in range and in capability). The latter make the possibility of waging a 'limited' nuclear war possible (although 'limited' in effect may mean 'limited to Europe').

The 1970s were predominantly a decade of détente. SALT I was agreed in 1972; mutual, balanced force reductions were begun in 1973. The European security conference was held at Helsinki in 1975, and there was the promise of SALT II. Tension seemed to have eased. Then came Afghanistan in 1979 and the death of détente. Since then both sides have plunged further into the development of more sophisticated weapons. The so-called 'neutron bomb', with its capacity by initially enhanced radiation to kill people but not damage buildings, was offered as a more powerful deterrent. It was in fact rejected by the Carter administration though re-introduced by President Reagan.

SALT II was not ratified by the US Congress. In 1980 the NATO strategy was made public in President Carter's Presidential Directive number 59: 'flexible response' now included 'counterforce' – the capacity to make a nuclear attack on enemy nuclear installations. The key to counterforce is accuracy. It includes the possibility of a 'first use' of tactical theatre nuclear weapons (as distinct from a strategic 'first strike'). Pershing II and Cruise missiles are supposed to be part of the NATO flexible response and counterforce strategy.

In 1979 Chancellor Schmidt of West Germany called for NATO to respond to the build-up of Soviet SS 20s targeted against Europe. The NATO decision to deploy Pershing II and Cruise missiles was the result. Since then Mrs Thatcher's administration in London (with her call: 'We must match strength with strength') and President Reagan's in Washington have increasingly impressed on the public consciousness the view that the best form of deterrence is to look ready to go to war. The US government decided under pressure from Defense Secretary Caspar Weinberger to start production of the neutron weapon. *The Guardian* leader of 12 August 1981 commented: 'It is a fiction to say that it will not be deployed in Europe: it is useless anywhere else. This is a battlefield weapon par excellence, with a small yield and a range of some 70 miles from its intended launch vehicles. Whatever its value in deterrence theory it virtually promises nuclear response to a conventional attack, but on a scale small enough to ensure that continental America and continental Russia could, if they so agree, stay out of it.'

We are now witnessing a growing and ever more sophisticated network of increasingly threatening weapons. Side by side, although what is chicken and what is egg is very hard to say, we have a continually modified and increasingly intricate theory of deterrence.

Military-industrial complex

There is a further factor of major importance which underlies to a very large extent the changes and growth in deterrence theory and the escalation of nuclear arsenals in the
West. It was in 1961 in his farewell Presidential address to the
American people that Eisenhower made his now famous
speech about the 'military-industrial complex':

> Until the latest of our world conflicts, the United States
> had no armaments industry. American makers of plough-
> shares could, with time and as required, make swords as
> well. But now we can no longer risk emergency improvis-
> ation of national defense; we have been compelled to
> create a permanent armaments industry of vast propor-
> tions. ... This conjunction of immense military establish-
> ment and large arms industry is new in the American
> experience. The total influence – economic, political, even
> spiritual – is felt in every city, every statehouse, every office
> of federal government. Yet we must not fail to com-
> prehend its grave implications. Our toil, resources, and
> livelihood are all involved; so is the very structure of our
> society.
>
> In the councils of government we must guard against the
> acquisition of unwarranted influence, whether sought or
> unsought, by the military-industrial complex. The
> potential for the disastrous rise of misplaced power exists
> and will persist. We must never let the weight of this
> combination endanger our liberties or democratic pro-
> cesses.

The authors of *Defended to Death* are not alone in believing
that this is precisely what is happening. 'It seems that the
nature and volume of nuclear weapons are no longer determined by military 'needs' nor is military strategy any longer
under the control of political policies . . . the weapons have
acquired the power to dictate to their political masters.'[12]
They believe that the West is already in the grip of a

frictionless spiralling of nuclear arms development in which official political policy is fed into the 'Steel Triangle' of military, academic and industrial interests, and emerges in terms of overdevelopment of actual needs, which are then given *post-factum* justification by the politicians who have to find money to pay for them. They then become the basis for future policy, future research and development, future vested interests in the military-industrial complex, future needs for *post-factum* justification. The spiral, they believe, is self-winding. The arms race can only escalate. We now have a permanent 'war economy'. It is easy to see, given this viewpoint, how policies are understood as subordinate to weapons, and how strategies can be created to contain the weapons being made.

However right these authors are in their analysis, what is unmistakably clear is that 'deterrence' has become the overarching defence theory under which everything is at present subordinated – at least in the West. (There are recent hints that in the minds of some strategists, the increasing accuracy of 'battlefield' nuclear weapons makes war-fighting not only thinkable but actively to be planned for. And there are very recent moves in the US to move beyond deterrence towards Western control of space by particle-beam and laser weapons. The intention of these would be to eliminate Soviet attacking missiles in the air before they reached their target. Whether such drawing-board proposals could ever serve to stabilize – or would only further destabilize – international relations, can only be guessed at. There are further recent suggestions from some scientists that a major nuclear exchange could result in a carbon dust cloud so dense that it would cause a sudden lowering of the Earth's temperature with catastrophic (ice age) results lasting for many months. If such suggestions are confirmed, no doubt they have a significant effect on deterrence theory.)

The viewpoint of the British government, expressed in 1981 by the then Defence Secretary John Nott, confirms NATO deterrence strategy in these terms:

It is quite clear that any war fought with modern weapons – conventional as well as nuclear – would cause immense suffering. That is why we in the UK, together with our NATO allies, have adopted the strategy of deterrence. Our objective is to make it clear to a potential aggressor that the risks he would incur would be out of all proportion to any gains he might hope to make. I cannot emphasise too strongly that this strategy is intended to prevent war by demonstrating that an attack on NATO is simply not worthwhile . . . .

NATO is a purely defensive alliance and has no aggressive intentions towards any country. We cannot, however, ignore the threat to our security and freedom posed by the Warsaw Pact, and especially the Soviet Union who have a large arsenal of nuclear and conventional forces, far more than could reasonably be required for defence. The invasion of Afghanistan is only the latest demonstration that the Soviet Union are willing to use their military strength to achieve political ends. While NATO does not need to match the Warsaw Pact weapon-for-weapon, we do need a range of forces, nuclear and conventional, so as to be able to defend ourselves from any level of attack. By showing this we aim to prevent any aggression against us in the first place.[13]

The case for NATO's continuing balance of terror policy was also put recently by former Chief of the Defence Staff Sir Neil Cameron in the symposium *What Hope in an Armed World?*[14] Sir Neil believes that the global strategic balance has achieved some stability, though he comments on the Soviet Union's 'opportunistic approach to the changing world scene', and that the Soviet Union must be seen as the prospective enemy. 'So much of a threat to world peace lies in the fact that the West as such cannot send a concerted signal to the USSR that their expansionist policies and their restriction on human rights may eventually lead to an East-West confrontation and possibly war by miscalculation.' He quotes

Zbigniew Brzezinski in support of the view that the Soviet Union as such is beginning to break up, and what is emerging may well be a sense of Russian nationalism. The economic, agricultural and oil needs of the USSR all contribute to their present instability.

In such circumstances, says Sir Neil, we must have an effective and credible deterrent. He quotes Sir Arthur Hockaday: 'The more easily one can conceive of a decision actually being taken to use a particular weapon, the more seriously that weapon will be regarded by a potential aggressor and the more credible will be our overall posture of deterrence. Consequently it will be less likely that war will actually break out or that the weapons will ever have to be used.'[15]

Deterrence is about the prevention of war – the prevention of all war, because 'some outbreak of conventional war between the Superpowers could easily become nuclear when one side or the other starts to lose'.[16] Sir Neil believes that unilateral British nuclear disarmament would leave Britain wide open to Soviet blackmail. The perception that the Soviets now have some nuclear superiority over the West and that a 'window of vulnerability' remains open, has led to the US determination in recent years on a hard target force. Our guard, insists Sir Neil, must be kept up until multilateral nuclear disarmament can be negotiated. 'There is no doubt in my mind that until we can persuade the Soviet Union to disarm and enter freely into the family of nations, we must maintain our nuclear deterrent.'[17]

Such confidence – if not complacency – in maintaining the balance of terror is not shared, however, by all military commentators. Indeed, there seems to be a growing unease about current deterrence strategy. Former Chief of Defence Staff Field Marshal Lord Carver, for example, has added his voice to those of other military strategists calling for a 'No First Strike' commitment from NATO. Writing in *The Tablet* in December 1982, Lord Carver noted that the Russians have made a declaration that they would never use nuclear weapons first. NATO has refused to make such a declaration on the grounds that the threat implied in keeping open the option of 'first use' is essential to deter the Soviet Union with its preponderant strength in conventional forces from launching a conventional attack on Western Europe. While there are some strategists who believe that a nuclear war could be fought and won because it could be kept 'limited', and others who believe that the possibility of keeping the option of 'first use' open is essential to deterrence, there are others like Lord Carver who believe that a NATO declaration of 'no first use' would provide a breakthrough which could result in significant arms reduction. 'The more acceptable nuclear war may appear to be to governments and military men of the nuclear powers, the more likely it is that it will actually come about.'

To give another example, *The Guardian* of 21 June 1983 reported the remarks of the chairman of NATO's military committee, Canadian Admiral Robert Falls: 'If arms control talks don't work, then it might become necessary to act unilaterally to reduce especially battlefield nuclear weapons, because we have perhaps more than we need.' A cautious, diplomatically phrased comment, but one which betrays unease at the highest levels with the 'progress' of the 'arms race'.

Thirdly, in his 1979 speech to the Stockholm Peace Research Institute, Earl Mountbatten spoke of his sadness that there seems so little evidence that those responsible for the 'disastrous course' of the arms race are 'reaching for the brakes'. He has never found the idea of a 'limited' theatre nuclear exchange credible. 'As a military man I could see no use for any nuclear weapons which would not end in escalation, with consequences that no one can conceive. ... I cannot imagine a situation in which nuclear weapons would be used as battlefield weapons without the conflagration spreading.'

He then asked how steps could be taken to make sure that these things never come about, steps for achieving practical measures of nuclear arms control and disarmament. 'The real need is for both sides to replace the attempts to maintain a balance through ever-increasing and ever more costly nuclear armaments by a balance based on mutual restraint.' The nuclear arms race, he said, has 'no military purpose'. 'There are powerful voices around the world who still give credence to the old Roman precept: if you desire peace, prepare for war. This is absolute nuclear nonsense and I repeat, it is a disastrous misconception to believe that by increasing the total uncertainty one increases one's own certainty.' He concluded with the plea that 'someone, somewhere will take the first step along the long stony road which will lead us to an effective form of nuclear arms limitation, including the banning of Tactical Nuclear Weapons. . . . The world now stands on the brink of the final abyss. Let us all resolve to take all practical steps to ensure that we do not, through our own folly, go over the edge.'[18]

Here is apocalyptic language from a military man of world stature. As the then Archbishop of York, Dr Stuart Blanch, said at the General Synod debate on the Report *The Church and the Bomb* in February 1983: 'We are talking about the end of the world, and how to avert it.' Our theological foundation needs to be broad enough to encompass viewpoints like these.

What, then, are the theological issues which our frightened new world forces us to consider? Here are some of them.

We need in the first place to make an adequate political judgment about the nature of potential aggressors against whom we need to make precautions of defence. In the context of East-West tension, this means a realistic appraisal as far as is possible of Soviet foreign policy towards the West. We need to make a judgment about the moral status of Western and Communist social systems, and decide whether 'Western democracies for all their failings (to which no one can be blind) embody values which lie closer to the Christian vision than does Soviet totalitarianism'.[18] Does our understanding of the nature of man from a Christian perspective lead us to the view that a democratic system with checks and balances in the uses of power provides a better context for the development of moral responsibility and godliness than does totalitarianism? We need to make a judgment about the 'structurally ungodly' nature of Soviet intentions. The authors of *Protest and Perish*[20], for example, argue forcefully that Russia was and remains an expansionist power, that Soviet leaders regard national independence as a 'bourgeois myth' and that the recent expansion of Soviet influence into Hungary (1956), Czechoslovakia (1968) and Afghanistan (1979) is evidence of a continuing commitment to use military force to attain their declared objective of world domination. They quote a USSR education textbook in elementary military training which states that their children may be called on to fight a war against 'imperialism': 'This war in its essence and political content will be the decisive armed conflict of the two opposing world systems.' These authors note that the Soviet leaders not only regard nuclear war as not unthinkable, but encourage their population to believe that such a war can be won.

The opposing political judgment (for example in *Defended to Death*) sees the Soviet involvement in Prague and Kabul not in terms of expansionism, but rather in terms of their perceived threat to the security of their borders, and a defensive policy of creating buffer states around them.

A Christian moral judgment will thus need to consider both the moral status of the two 'world systems', and also the weight to be placed on the 'Soviet threat'. This will take us into consideration of the nature and trustworthiness of man, and the function of the state in the purposes of God. What values does the state exist to preserve? What is the state's authority and power? What means may the state use to safeguard its existence and its values?

Secondly, we will need to make a theological and moral judgment about deterrence. What is involved in making a threat of massive retaliation if our nation is attacked? Is this a morality of bluff, or of deceit? Is this a morality of *intending* to do what it would be immoral *actually* to do? Can it be right ever to take a decision which could result in the ending of all

83

possibility of future life for the societies which are engaged in deterrence precisely for their survival and protection? Yet can it ever be right to leave all nuclear power in the hands of those who might have no scruples about its use? How is a Christian to judge an appropriate response to nuclear blackmail?

Thirdly, we will need to keep in mind the apocalyptic dimensions to this issue, as outlined, for example, by Lord Mountbatten and Archbishop Blanch. Where are we to draw the lines between areas which are open for human decision, and areas which belong properly only to the providence of God? How are we to make our personal and political decisions in the light of the fact that this is God's world, and that Christ is his coming King?

The next part of our book will sketch out a theological foundation on which we can then try to build a Christian moral response to these and other questions.

Notes for chapter five

[1]Second Vatican Council, 'Avoidance of War' in *Gaudium et Spes* (December 1965), chapter V section 1 in A. Flannery (ed.), *The Conciliar and Post-Conciliar Documents* (Fowler Wright Books Ltd., 1981), p.988.

[2]*The Medical Consequences of Nuclear Weapons* (Medical Campaign Against Nuclear Weapons, 1982).

[3]*Ibid.*, p.37.

[4]BMA's Board of Science and Education, *The Medical Effects of Nuclear War* (John Wiley, 1983), p.124.

[5]H. Thielicke, *Theological Ethics*, 2 (English Translation, Eerdmans, 1969), p.419f.

[6]*Ibid.*, p.426.

[7]Sir Neil Cameron in Richard Harries (ed.), *What Hope in an Armed World?* (Pickering & Inglis, 1982), p.17.

[8]P. Towle, I. Elliot and G. Frost, *Protest and Perish* (Institute for European Defence and Strategic Studies, 1982), p.46.

[9]I am indebted for much of the following documentation, though not necessarily the argument, to G. Prins (ed.), *Defended to Death* (Penguin, 1983).

[10]Hansard 537, 1 March 1955, col.1898–9.

[11]G. Prins (ed.), *op.cit.*, p.92.

[12]*Ibid.*, p.133.

[13]John Nott (British Defence Secretary) Personal letter to the author, Jan. 1981.

[14]Sir Neil Cameron in Richard Harries (ed.), *op.cit.*, ch.1.

[15]*Ibid.*

[16]*Ibid.*

[17]*Ibid.*

[18]Reprinted in *Third Way*, **4** (8), September 1980.

[19]F. Bridger, *The Cross and the Bomb: Christian Ethics and the Nuclear Debate* (Mowbrays, 1983), p.42.

[20]P. Towle, *op.cit.*

Part 3_____

Putting down markers — towards a theological foundation

Introduction

We can now see that the question about 'the biblical approach to war' does not yield a straightforward answer. The answer is complicated in at least two sorts of ways.

First, as with practically all ethical decision-making, we are faced not with the simple application of a principle to a problem (as though 'Thou shalt not kill' settled the issue). We are faced rather with a complex of principles, often in conflict with each other, related to a range of interconnected problems. Neither the biblical examples nor the history of Christian tradition give us straightforward answers to today's questions. So our questions will have to take the form: Does the Bible give us guidance about ethical decision-making in a complex world? Can biblical theology help us make sense of the complexities and the conflicts, as well as help us towards Christian ways of approaching the ethical questions these raise? I believe that it can, and this is our concern in Chapter 6.

We will try first to make a theological assessment of the nature of ethical decision-making in this fallen world 'after the flood'. This will point us back to God's purposes in creation, and to his covenant. It will face us with the reality of human sin and demonic power. It will confront us with the gospel of Christ and his kingdom. Christian ethics, we will argue, is an ethic of allegiance to God, and in this context we will spend some time on the teaching of the Sermon on the Mount as it relates to our theme. (This will give us opportunity to reflect further on the Christian pacifist's case.)

We will also indicate how the radical demands of the kingdom have to be held in tension with God's other requirements and provisions for order and justice within the fallen world. We end with a consideration of what Helmut Thielicke calls the 'ethical borderline', in which, at the extremities of moral conflict, no ways open to us are good, and yet moral decisions have to be taken.

Our answer is complex in a second way also. As we saw in our brief sketch of recent history, the question of war, and especially the questions of modern technological warfare, are raising wholly new issues. In Chapter 8, therefore, we will be focusing especially on the background to the question of war, bearing in mind in particular some of the new issues with which our modern world is faced. The question 'Why are there wars?' can be approached first in terms of the nature of man, and the fact that – as the UNESCO charter puts it – 'wars begin in the minds of men'. We will explore the nature of the human predicament from a theological perspective, looking at the 'sanctity' of life, and the nature of human aggression. This will take us on to Chapter 9 and an exploration of God's order and ours, God's justice and ours, and the meaning of 'peace'.

The question 'Why are there wars?' could also be answered in terms of political structures and societies which have values they think are worth fighting for. In other words, we need to make a theological evaluation of the nature, authority and limits of the modern sovereign state. So in Chapter 10 we will try to form a picture of the way the Bible understands the state, and see what links may be made to our modern world. We will then have to ask about the propriety of the state's involvement in war, which will lead us back to the 'just war' theory. Finally we will remind ourselves that in our world context, the issues of war have been sharpened considerably since, for example, the days of Luther. In our world where mutual genocide is on the agenda, we are faced much more starkly than earlier generations with the wide apocalyptic dimensions of our decision-making; with the nature and destiny of humanity, and of the environment in which God has put us; and with the very survival of 'society' at all. How, in all this, do we discern and live in the light of the providence of God?

That theological agenda is our task in Part 3, and then in Part 4 we will try to build on this foundation some moral guidelines about war, especially nuclear war, and nuclear deterrence.

6 The shape of Christian ethics

One of the over-arching themes of biblical theology is God's covenant of grace. In the Bible God is depicted as a covenant-making, covenant-restoring, covenant-fulfilling God. From the time of God's dealings with Abraham (Gn.17:2), through the pivotal exodus events of Passover and Sinai at the time of Moses (Ex.2:24; 6:5; 19:5ff.), the ratification of covenant with the people under Joshua (Jos.2:1–28), the establishment of a covenant with David (Ps.89:28) and the promise of a renewed covenant in some of the prophetic writings (Je.31:33; cf. Ezk.36:26ff.), to the giving of the cup of the covenant by Jesus to his disciples in the Upper Room (Mt.26:27ff.), we find that God establishes his people in covenant relationship with himself. The covenant is God's initiative of grace ('I will be your God') coupled with his invitation and his command ('You shall be my people'). This covenant refrain can be found again and again in the Old Testament. It is the theme of God's dealings with his people to the close of the age (Rev.21:3,7). God the creator is willing to be known as 'our God'; the invitation, demand and promise is that we should be 'his people'.

To give a gross oversimplification of themes which have been the subject of much theological disagreement, we could say that in summary biblical ethics has the shape of 'covenant ethics' superimposed on 'creation ethics'. Both Old and New Testaments relate ethical demands to the facts of creation: that we are creatures of God and so accountable to him as Creator. Both Old and New Testaments also relate ethical behaviour to the sort of God God is, namely that he is a God of redemptive grace, who makes himself known as 'our God' and invites our response. It is in this covenant context that we should understand the category of 'law'. The 'torah', or fatherly instruction of God to his covenant people in the Old Testament, is the pattern of life appropriate for people who are called to be 'his'. At Sinai, for example, God reminds the people of his grace: 'I am the LORD your God, who brought you out of the land of Egypt' (Ex.20:2) and then gives them his law: 'You shall have no other gods before me' (Ex.20:3ff.). Likewise the narrative of Exodus 34 recounts God's initiative (verses 6–7), and then Moses' response of loyalty and allegiance (verse 9).

There is, in other words, a pattern of life appropriate for covenant people. It is expressed in the covenant rule 'You shall be holy; for I the LORD your God am holy' (Lv.19:2). This is a theme elaborated in the teaching of Jesus: 'You, therefore, must be perfect, as your heavenly Father is perfect' (Mt.5:48); and by his apostle: 'As he who called you is holy, be holy yourselves in all your conduct' (1 Pet.1:15).

It is in this covenant setting that we understand the Torah both as a description of the character of the holy God, and also of the pattern of life appropriate to his people. The Torah specifies what 'holy living' means in certain contexts. It gives guidance to the covenant people in their calling to 'love the LORD their God' and to 'love their neighbours as themselves' (Dt.6:5; Lv.19:18). The early Book of the Covenant (Ex.20:18 – 23:33), for example, details outworking of obedience to God in response to his covenant of grace in the problems of a desert-dwelling, bronze age community. The later Holiness Code of Leviticus 17–26 concentrated on requirements of ritual purity needed to express something of the nature of 'holy living', as well as providing for ritual sacrificial expiation of sin. The Deuteronomic restatement of the Torah fills out the religious basis and character of Mosaic legislation, deriving law from the acts of God's redemption and the nature of his character (chapters 1–11), and holding together social and personal ethics in terms, not of mere 'obedience' to a code of laws, but as 'walking in God's ways' (8:6; 10:12), of 'cleaving' to him (10:20), of living as his 'sons' (14:1) and especially of 'loving' him (6:4f.). The law, in other words, is seen as God's generous gift in order that the people should enjoy God's covenanted provisions for them – 'that it may go well' with them (5:33).

The covenant ethic then, is not primarily an ethic merely of obedience to law; it is much more an *ethics of allegiance* to the covenant God, who has taken the initiative to come towards his people in redeeming grace. Furthermore, as the covenant rule makes clear (You shall be holy, as I am holy), the people in their human relationships – in their covenants of life with life, in their dealings with each other, in their families, in their social life and institutions – are to express something of the character of their covenant God. Ethical allegiance then becomes obedience to God's loving word, in order to express something of his holy character.

The covenant with Noah
Behind and before all the specific covenants of God with his people to which we have just referred, however, the Bible has the story of a more fundamental covenant still: that between God and 'every living creature'. The story is that of God's covenant with Noah after the flood. This story most vividly reminds us that the covenant of God is made, and his law given, in the setting of a disordered and fallen world. It reminds us that to some extent, God's law is an accommodation of God's perfect will to the conditions of the fallen world.

deals with his world. No longer is the command of God straightforward as it was in the Garden. In that story, there was no hint of a death penalty: there was no hint of murder. But in Genesis 9 we have a recognition both of murder, and of a command of God to restrain such evil by the provision of penalties. The law of God in the covenant described in the story of Noah, in other words, is a law which is 'modified' by, or refracted by, or appropriate to, the needs of a disordered world. This is not something, as it were, forced on God. God in his sovereign majesty calls 'every living creature' into the covenant of his restored creation, and decrees the conditions under which human life shall be lived.

So when we come to the expression of God's law later on in the story of specific covenants made with Abraham, Moses, and so on, we need to keep in mind this double aspect to the will of God. There is a divine command, that we be holy as he is holy; there is also a provision of God for the restraint of evil in the fallen world.

The Decalogue itself illustrates this double aspect. On the one hand it requires the worship of only one God; on the other hand it acknowledges the temptation to make graven images. It requires the honour of God's name, and respect for the sabbath, while acknowledging that both can be disregarded. The negative tone of the commandments against murder, adultery, theft, false witness and coveting have the sense both of obligation and of penalty. The law is occasioned by and relevant to a fallen world. It is, as it were, an 'emergency' provision of God's grace, necessary because of sin.

In many of the more specific commands of the Pentateuch, regulating the life of the desert community, there is both the straight command 'You shall . . . you shall not . . .' and also the casuistic legislation 'If this happens, then . . .'. Through all this is to be seen both the nature of the requirement of the covenant of God which his people need to discern in order to give appropriate expression to their allegiance, and also the 'emergency' provisions of God's 'refracted' or 'provisional' will which are to order the lives of fallen people and to restrain evil.

We can also find a recognition of this double aspect to 'God's will' in the New Testament, most clearly, perhaps, in the narrative of Jesus' discussion with the Pharisees about divorce (Mt.19:3ff.). Jesus indicated that there was a distinction between the *permission* of God for a bill of divorce granted 'for your hardness of heart' (Mt.19:8; *cf.* Dt.24:1ff.), and the *will* of God in the perfection of creation ('from the beginning it was not so', Mt.19:8, referring back in Mt.19:4,5 to Gn.1:27 and 2:24). God the Creator in his loving providence makes certain rulings for this fallen world, even though they are far from his creation intention. There are two aspects to God's will: his 'perfect will' (which Jesus embodied and taught), and his 'provisional will for the fallen world', by which God deals with the brokenness and disorder of men and society in which hearts are hard. By the fact that the bill of divorce in Deuteronomy 24 was apparently given to restrain male cruelty and maximize justice even in divorce, we can see that this 'emergency' provision was given to bring even the brokenness of sin back as far as possible to the Creator's pattern.

Now this distinction between God's 'perfect' and 'provisional' will is crucially important, especially when we come in a later section to try to interpret the Sermon on the Mount. If we fail to understand the ambiguity of this age in which God requires of us covenant allegiance, we may fall over into inaccurate pictures of the reality of human life in the fallen world. On the one hand, we might take the radical demands of the Sermon on the Mount as a new law appropriate for all life in this age. This would be to deal with this present age as though it still existed in its original unfallen state, or as though the coming Day of the Lord had already dawned and all creation had already been made new. As we shall see, we cannot understand the Sermon on the Mount in these terms.

On the other hand, we might mistake the 'provisional' expression of the will of God for the fallen world as in fact an

It reminds us that we live in a state of tension.

After the destruction of the world by the waters in God's judgment against evil, man is offered a new beginning under the rainbow. He is again offered a world in which to live, over which to have dominion, and in which to exercise his stewardship. He is again commanded to be fruitful and multiply and fill the earth (Gn.9:1).

So much is reminiscent of the creation story itself. But the tone is different. No longer is the context 'very good' (Gn.1:31); rather the world is full of 'fear' and 'dread' (Gn.9:2). This new start is 'marked from the outset with the stigma of the breach of covenant'.[1] The sin of man, recorded in Genesis 3, has led to the growth of aggressive cruelty between men (Gn.4), to the universal rule of death (the constant refrain of Gn.5), and demonic wickedness (Gn.6:1–4)[2], leading to the assessment: 'every imagination of the thoughts of [man's] heart was only evil continually' (Gn.6:5).

The judgment of the flood is God's response to pervasive evil (Gn.6:7). But now, after the flood, the story continues with God's re-establishment of the conditions under which life may again be lived. Dominion, however, is no longer simply granted; it has to be struggled for (Gn.9:2). Furthermore, there is now need for legal constraints on the life of man. For the first time, God's law contains a note of restraint and punishment: 'Whoever sheds the blood of man, by man shall his blood be shed' (Gn.9:6). This new world, after the fall, and after the judgment of the flood, is a disordered world needing a legally imposed order. Here, then, are the beginnings of a doctrine of social restraint necessary because of the wickedness of fallen men. This is the beginning of a concept which later develops into a doctrine of the state. There is a specific provision of God for the fallen world for the restraint of evil, and the ordering of the life of man.

What we are beginning to see in this story is a recognition that the fall of man has to some extent changed the way God expression of God's creation intention. This would be to understand the state, for example, as an order of creation, instead of as an emergency provision for the fallen world, a limited providential restraint necessary because of sin. The extreme of this view might be that war, as an expression of the policies of the state, could then become sanctified as 'the will of God'. This would be the inclination of the militarist crusading tendency in some aspects of 'warlike' Christianity. The best we may say is that war, if justified at all, can only be seen as part of an emergency and limited provision of God for the fallen world.[3] But to this we shall return.

In summary so far, therefore, 'covenant ethics' are set in the context of the tensions of a fallen world; the question posed by covenant ethics is how best to give expression within this fallen world to our allegiance to the covenant God who has called us to express something of his holy character.

The demonic

One further factor which the story of the flood highlights (Gn.6:5ff.) is the contrast between the *goodness* of God's creation (Gn.1:31) and the greatness of the *evil* in which man became enmeshed. The earth has become corrupt and filled with violence (Gn.6:11). Through the attempt to organize itself on the basis of an abandonment of the will of God, the sinister possibilities of evil within man and between men become disclosed. And the picture we are given, from Genesis 3 onwards, is that in and behind the evil in the heart of men a demonic evil power is concealed.

In our day, the increasingly rapid processes of secularization, which call in question the Christian view of supernatural reality and of a world held in being by the providence of God, are our attempts to organize and constitute our world order exclusively on the basis of our human autonomies. As Thielicke comments: 'As a result, we have been able for the first time to see clearly what the world really is. To be sure its most sinister possibilities have not yet been fully unleashed. However, we are beginning to get some idea of the monstrous nature of its demonic potential, and we have the sneaking suspicion that the visions in the Johannine apocalypse are not too far removed from reality. Hence it is not by accident that there has developed among us a new readiness to take demonic powers seriously.'[4]

The basic question, in other words, concerns our contemporary crisis over the concept of reality. How are we to understand the demand and will of God within this world? Do we believe that 'the world', human society organized without reference to God, hides the presence of supernatural evil? How are we to frame our Christian ethics in the context of what Thielicke calls 'the demonization of the world'?

The two aeons: Adam and Christ

When we turn over to the New Testament, we find a continuation, a clarification and a deepening of the themes we have so far explored: the allegiance of faith in the tensions of a fallen world. One of the clearest sections is the second half of Romans 5 where Paul sets Adam and Christ in juxtaposition. To quote Anders Nygren:

Paul thinks in terms of two aeons. Two realms stand over against each other. One is the dominion of *death* over all that is human, the age of Adam. The other is the dominion of *life*, the age of Christ. . . . Paul is not working with our usual categories of time and history here, saying that all before Christ's birth were 'in Adam'. No, he is speaking of two different *orders of existence*. Outside of Christ, in Adam, the world and human life is in bondage to the rule of Death. In Christ, and supremely in his resurrection, the new age of Life has burst upon the world. Jesus stands, then, at the frontier of the ages, and those who are 'in Christ' stand with him. 'If any one is in Christ, he is a new creation; the old has passed away, behold, the new has come' (2 Cor.5:17). This is Paul's Gospel: In Christ, God has brought something wholly new into our midst – the new Age of Life.[5]

From Romans 5, the analysis of our present world order confirms what we said earlier: this world, left to itself, 'stands under the sovereign dominion of death'.[6] Through Christ, God has burst in upon this world with the dominion of life, calling us by the gospel to enter into it with him.

In the Gospels, the language is different, but the theme is the same. Jesus' preaching of 'the kingdom' picks up the language of Old Testament Messianic promise, and says that the blessings of Messiah's salvation are now present in this world. The kingdom is present in the divine activity of the king. The parables of the kingdom illustrate the dynamic concept of an active, ruling God. The kingdom has already dawned in Jesus.

But both in Paul's writings, and in Jesus' teaching of the kingdom, there is a double thrust. Paul speaks of the coming 'Day of Christ': he says 'we await a Saviour' (Phil.3:20); he says that 'salvation is nearer to us now than when we first believed; the night is far gone, the day is at hand' (Rom.13:11–12). In the Gospels, there is on the one hand an emphasis on *present fulfilment* in Jesus (Mt.12:28: 'the kingdom of God has come upon you'; Mt.25:34: 'inherit the kingdom'), and on the other hand an emphasis on *future consummation* (Mt.8:11: 'many will come ...'; Mt.19:28: 'in the new world ...'; Mt.6:10: 'Thy kingdom come ...').

In other words *there is a 'not yet' as well as a 'now'* to salvation. God's kingdom *will come* at the end of the age in a mighty irruption into history, inaugurating the perfect order of the age to come. But God's kingdom *has already come* into history in the person and mission and death and resurrection of Jesus.

So once again we return to the thought that Christian living (the life of the kingdom) and therefore Christian ethics (the ethics of the kingdom) take place within the tension of the aeons, within the tension between the 'now' and the 'not yet'. Although the Christian's orientation is different – he is a new creature in Christ – he still lives within the constraints of the fallen and 'demonized' world. The New Testament metaphors of Christian warfare will still need to be taken utterly seriously in the continuing struggle to live the new life within the constraints of the old.

In this struggle, the presence of the Holy Spirit is promised as a divine resource. In the New Testament much more clearly than in the Old, we can have (as indeed the covenant models in their own ways also indicate) that what God requires, that in grace by his Spirit he also gives. Torah ethics then become, as it were, 'swallowed up' into Spirit ethics. The Holy Spirit begins to make a reality, through the 'harvesting' of his 'fruit' (Gal.5:22), the divine requirement that we 'be holy' (*cf*. 1 Pet.1:15). The promise of the prophets of old begins to become true that God will 'put my spirit within you, and cause you to walk in my statutes and be careful to observe my ordinances' (Ezk.36:27). Here is the renewed covenant in which God will 'put my law within them, and I will write it upon their hearts' (Je.31:33). But the work of the Spirit is a process of growth. His weapons are given to us for Christian warfare in that struggle towards being 'holy'.

Notes for chapter six

[1]H. Thielicke (notes from unpublished lectures).
[2]G. von Rad in *Genesis* (English Translation, SCM, 1961), p.110, writes, 'These angelic beings let themselves be enticed by the beauty of human women to grievous sin; they fall from their ranks and mix with them in wild licentiousness.'
[3]H. Thielicke (notes from unpublished lectures).
[4]H. Thielicke, *Theological Ethics*, **1** (English Translation, Eerdmans, 1969), p.4.
[5]A. Nygren, *Commentary on Romans* (English Translation, Fortress Press, 1949), p.20.
[6]*Ibid.*, p.26.

7 Approaching the Sermon on the Mount

It is now time to concentrate our attention more specifically on the ethical teaching of Jesus, particularly that drawn together for us in Matthew chapter 5. The antitheses of the second half of that chapter: 'You have heard that it was said . . . but I say to you . . .' include the essential charter of Christian pacifism in verse 39: 'Do not resist one who is evil', and verse 44: 'Love your enemies'. It is now time to examine these carefully.

We have already indicated in Chapter 2 that there are many different approaches to the interpretation of the Sermon on the Mount. Our task now will be to make clear our own approach. We will need both to examine the exegesis of the texts and also to try to interpret them in the light of their setting in Matthew's Gospel, and in the light of our wider theological perspective. This will then enable us to make a fuller assessment of relevant parts of the Christian pacifist's case.

There is a long-standing tradition of interpretation which sees the arrangement of Matthew's Gospel, his Christian Manifesto written primarily with Jewish readers in mind, as a conscious echo of the arrangement of the Pentateuch. The significance of 'the Mount' (5:1: Jesus 'went up . . . the mountain'), and Jesus' posture seated as rabbi or legislator, both seem strongly to parallel the giving of the law through Moses at Mount Sinai. How much we are intended to make of the coming of Christian faith in terms of a New Exodus, and to see Jesus as a New Moses, the mediator of a New Covenant, is not really clear in Matthew's presentation. But that Jesus is giving his own word in the context of a Judaistic understanding of the teaching of Moses is unmistakably clear. Perhaps W. D. Davies' summary is the most helpful:

> [Jesus] is not Moses come as Messiah ... so much as Messiah, Son of Man, Emmanuel, who has absorbed the Mosaic function. The Sermon on the Mount is therefore ambiguous: suggestive of the Law of a New Moses, it is also the authoritative word of the Lord, the Messiah: it is the Messianic Torah.[1]

We do not have a Jesus set in opposition to Moses, rather a Jesus who is the *fulfilment* of what Moses was. Yet we need to say even more than that. We need to say first that the teaching of Jesus certainly does confront us as torah: there is a moral imperative to be obeyed. Jesus is teaching his disciples (verse 1) the pattern of life and character which is appropriate for members of 'the kingdom of heaven' (verses 3, 10, 19, 20). The disciples of the kingdom of heaven are to 'be perfect' as their Father in heaven is perfect (5:48). They are to 'seek first his kingdom and his righteousness' (6:33).

So chapter 5 verses 17–48 spell out in some detail the character and the way of life by which this 'righteousness' is expressed. This is the way the disciples of the kingdom live. Here is no abolition of the requirements of the torah (verse 18). Here rather is a righteousness far more radical than the righteousness of the scribes and the Pharisees (verse 20). This is kingdom life.

Secondly, we must not separate the words of Jesus from Jesus himself. Elsewhere Matthew points us to his own understanding of the meaning of faith in terms of reliance on the authority of Jesus and his word (8:10; 8:13; 9:2; 9:22; 9:28ff.). And here we are directly confronted with Jesus' authority set over against the scribal interpretations of the law. 'You have heard that it was said . . .', even, 'You have understood literally what was said . . .' (verses 21, 27, 31, 33, 38, 43) – in which Jesus is referring to scribal interpretations of, and sometimes additions to, the Old Testament torah. 'But I say to you . . .' (verses 22, 28, 32, 34, 39, 44). The teaching here is not one more interpretation alongside that of the scribes. Here we are confronted with the moral imperative of Jesus' own words. The ethical command is at the same time the command to acknowledge the authority of Jesus, and also to trust him. As Davies says, 'And this can be so because in his every activity (3:15) and in his words (5:17f.) Jesus in his own character has fulfilled (i.e. brought to its destined end), the righteousness of which he speaks.'[2]

Thirdly, as Davies also says, we must read the Sermon on the Mount in its context in Matthew's Gospel:

It occurs after 4:23–25, which reveal the compassion of the

ministry of Jesus, how he went about not only preaching and teaching, but 'healing every disease and every infirmity among the people', and how 'they brought him all the sick, those afflicted with various diseases and pains, demoniacs, epileptics, and paralytics', and how 'he healed them'. The same emphasis on the mercy of his acts re-emerges in miracles in chapters 8–9; which follow the Sermon on the Mount. Before and after the demand of the Sermon stands the compassion of the Messiah. The infinite demand is embedded in infinite succour: they both belong together: his acts and his words are congruous. The words of Jesus the Messiah bring us to the climax of God's demand, but they do this in the context of a ministry which is the expression of the ultimate mercy.'[3]

In other words, as always with the dealings of God with his people, law is given in the context of grace. What God requires, that in Christ he also gives.

So what, in Jesus' teaching here, does God require? In what does 'kingdom life' consist? Matthew 5:17–48, in conscious dependence on the Ten Commandments, illustrate the radical nature of the meaning of God's law, and they do so by contrasting Jesus' teaching with the scribal interpretations of some Old Testament texts. We must not say that the Old Testament is concerned with outward behaviour and Jesus is concerned with inner motives (as a quick reading of verses 21 and 22, or 27 and 28 might suggest). The Old Testament was also concerned with inner motive, and indeed it is impossible to separate out ethical life from religious life in much of the Old Testament. What is going on here is a call to 'be perfect, as your heavenly Father is perfect' (verse 48), and that, in this context, is a challenge (as T. W. Manson[4] puts it) 'to produce words and deeds of a quality similar to that which we discern in those of the Master, and to follow him' (cf. Mt.19:21).

To follow Christ – that is what Christian ethics asks of us. And, as Manson says, 'To follow Christ is not to go in pursuit of an ideal, but to share in the results of an achieve-ment'.[5] What these antitheses offer, therefore, are concrete illustrations of what 'kingdom life', of what 'following Christ', would mean in certain situations. Jesus shows what would be really involved in living as a disciple of the kingdom – what would be really involved in loving our neighbour as ourself. And he shows it in thought, and word and deed. These teachings in the Sermon, in other words, have been embodied and lived out in the life and ministry of Jesus. We must not, therefore, make the Sermon into a new Law, more radical and demanding than Moses', as though by keeping these new laws we could fulfil the demands of the kingdom. That would land us straight into a new legalism more demanding than that of the Pharisees. It is rather that the ethical demands of the Law have become flesh and blood among us in Jesus. 'The Sermon is not saying: "This is how men in general should live if they really want to build the kingdom of God on earth". It is saying: "This is how you who are in the kingdom must live if your citizenship is to be a reality".'[6] This, then, is the pattern of life appropriate for disciples of the kingdom, appropriate for followers of Christ.

Let us look in particular now at the two antitheses central to our theme, that concerning retaliation (verses 38–42) and that concerning love for enemies (verses 43–48).

Verse 38 repeats the principle of Exodus 21:24, Leviticus 24:20 and Deuteronomy 19:21 (also known in other cultures, for example the Code of Hammurabi) that revenge and retaliation should be limited. The civil law provided for an exact compensation for an injury. This was an instruction for the judges of Israel, setting out the basis for justice, and restraining the bounds of punishment. It strictly limited the practice of blood revenge, by which members of a family tended to take the law into their own hands in retaliation for injury caused to one of them. In the course of justice in the courts of law, there was a strict principle of appropriate and limited retribution. However it seems that this principle was too easily transferred from the judicial context of just retribution to the altogether different context of personal relationships. And Jesus' words here reject this. He did not contradict the legal principle of just retribution appropriate for courts of law. What he did was to say that his disciples must not take that law into their own hands. In personal conduct, and in his attitude to his neighbours, the Christian must not behave according only to the principle of just retaliation.

In fact, as Hill comments[7], the verb *anthistemi*, translated 'resist' in verse 39, can mean 'oppose', even in the sense of 'oppose before a judge in a court of law'. On this interpretation, Jesus' teaching 'Do not resist one who is evil', means: in personal relationships, disciples are not to behave according to the principles of retribution appropriate to the courts, not even to assert their legal rights. There is to be a willingness not to retaliate and not to demand retribution. Members of the kingdom will not be exacting, but generous beyond the requirements of law.

This is the point of the four examples which follow (verses 39–42). If someone confronts you with insulting behaviour (strikes you on the right cheek), let him insult you again rather than seek reparation at law; if anyone would take you to court to sue you for your coat which he says belongs to him, surrender your cloak rather than demand reparation at law; if you are commandeered by a Roman soldier to carry his equipment for him for a mile, go further than the mere demands of the law; if someone asks you for a loan, do not turn away from him. 'Members of Christ's kingdom will be neither selfish nor exacting, but generous beyond what would normally be expected of them.'[8] The Christian, in other words, will not be ruled by the minimal demands of just retribution by constantly demanding legal rights. Even less will he take the law into his own hands. In personal relationships his attitudes will be marked by non-retaliation and a refusal to stand on rights.

This is by no means to say that the minimal requirements of judicial punishment, of the legal structures of law and retribution, and of the need to affirm legal rights, have themselves been done away with. This passage does not deny them, rather it presupposes them. We cannot argue from these examples of personal attitudes to any suggestion that the legal machinery of the state with its concern for justice in punishment, and its proper resistance of evil, must itself be rejected.

Verse 43 introduces a further antithesis, founded this time on Leviticus 19:18: 'You shall not take vengeance or bear any grudge against the sons of your own people, but you shall love your neighbour as yourself.' The Old Testament has no reference to 'hating enemies', and the interpretation of Jesus' words has led to much discussion. Who are the enemies whom he says are to be loved, and the persecutors who are to be prayed for? Hill's commentary quotes the advice of the *Manual of Discipline* of the Qumran community to 'love everyone whom God has elected and to hate everyone whom he has rejected . . . to hate all the sons of darkness'. Does 'enemy' here then mean, not a personal or political enemy, but an enemy of the faith, an enemy of the people of God? Would the early Christian community have perhaps been tempted to hate those who persecuted them? Or would this have been a reference to another scribal and Pharisaic tradition that 'love' should be shown to members of their own people but not to those who were outside the people of God? Could they have sought support for this view either from the 'holy war' tradition of early Israel's conflict with Canaan, or perhaps from some of the imprecatory Psalms?

Stott[9] examines both suggestions. He concludes with Bonhoeffer that there can be no more 'holy wars'. And he reminds us that the psalmist's 'hatred of evil' (*e.g.* Ps.139:19–24) is a proper and righteous hostility to the enemies of God, fired only by love for God's honour. It could not be used in any way as justification for hatred against personal or political enemies. No, the disciples of the kingdom must demonstrate the sort of love in action which reflects the generous and loving action of God. His love is not calculated in terms of worth or merit, but generously gives his sunshine and his rain to all (verse 45) by the operations of his 'common grace' irrespective of personal deserving. The motive for the disciples' love is to 'be sons of your Father who is in heaven'.

In personal relationships, therefore, these paragraphs teach us, the Christian is called to non-retaliation, and to generous love which goes beyond the demands of law.

The arguments of pacifism

In the light of this discussion, we must come back to the pacifist's case. It is based primarily on the example of Christ who, in Gethsemane and on the cross, refused the way of retaliation, and showed his love, even for personal enemies, in his willingness to lay down his rights, together with his life, and not seek retribution against evil. Furthermore, the Sermon on the Mount tells the disciples that this is to be their manner of life also in personal relationships.

However, these principles are then applied by the pacifist directly to the sphere of social ethics also. But as we have seen, we cannot extrapolate from the I-Thou encounter to the sphere of justice and the courts, nor from the personal one-to-one relationship to the activities of the state. Nor can we make the example and teaching of Christ into a new legalism for believers, let alone a new code of law for society as a whole. On the contrary, the Sermon *presupposes* the structures of law and of justice, and though the believer in his personal relationships is to go beyond the mere requirements of justice, he is not thereby excused from the task of upholding the principles of justice in civil society.

Indeed, once the focus of the question is broadened from the personal one-to-one encounter to include more than one neighbour, the application of this pattern of kingdom life becomes much more complicated. For if the 'one who is evil' is not confronting or insulting *me*, but is rather harming *someone for whom I have a responsibility of care* (perhaps the innocent child or the elderly or sick person), then for me to refuse to resist evil on their behalf, or to fail to see that the requirements of justice are met *for them,* would be to acquiesce in evil and even encourage it. In other words, when I am faced with a decision with respect to more than one neighbour, I am faced with adjudicating between the claims of neighbour love which may require different responses for different neighbours. It is precisely that adjudication between the different claims of neighbour love made on me by different neighbours that the principles of justice are there to serve. My love for my elderly sick neighbour will be expressed in a very different way from my love for our enemy. In order to care for the first I may in love *have* to resist the second.

The arguments of pacifism taken from the Sermon on the Mount, then, seem to involve an unwarranted extrapolation from the personal to the social, and from the claims of one neighbour to the claims of the wider society. But they are unwarranted in a deeper way still. What the claims of pacifism amount to is a view that the kingdom life to which the Sermon points can be equated with a pattern of social life which is attainable here and now. This fails to appreciate the tensions of the aeons to which we referred. It fails to see that the high demands of kingdom life are placed upon people who are also given over to 'hardness of heart'. It is a failure to recognize the deep disorder of the fallen world. It is a confusion of the 'not yet' with the 'now'.

While in the 'now', the Christian is called on to learn to express neighbour love in his relationships; he is also called on to work for that context of justice which is God's provision for the fallen world, until the 'not yet' dawns.

Whether the establishment of justice and the necessary resistance to evil done towards others can ever countenance the coercive use of force in war is of course another matter that we shall come to in a later chapter. But on that, the Sermon on the Mount does not have anything direct to say.

We shall in a later section look in more detail at the nature of justice, and at the relationship between justice and love.

Let us simply at this stage note that the word 'justice' is very close to that often translated 'righteousness' in contexts describing the righteous character of the covenant God. This is the righteousness of the King to which the Sermon on the Mount points us in its requirement that we seek first God's kingdom and his righteousness (Mt.6:33). The quest for justice in human relationships, we then see, is not far from the theme of the Sermon on the Mount.

Under the rainbow

Christian ethics, we have said, operates within a tension: a tension of the overlap of the 'aeons' (we are in Christ, but also still in Adam), and of the kingdom between its coming in Christ and its ultimate consummation at the Last Day. We have seen the radical demands of kingdom life illustrated in the Sermon on the Mount, and in terms of personal discipleship we have to learn, through the aid of the Holy Spirit, to express our life 'in Christ' by responding to situations of personal insult without retaliation, and replying to hatred and persecution with generous love. But that demand of 'kingdom life' is complicated in two ways. It is complicated within by the fact of our continuing 'in Adam', so that our discipleship is to be seen in terms of struggle and Christian warfare. It is complicated also when we move from the claims of one neighbour to the claims of a wider society.

It is here that we come up against the reality of the disordered structure of our world. The tensions of the aeons which we feel personally, are also tensions inherent in the structures of our social life. So the task of seeking to adjudicate in justice between competing claims, itself is beset by the pressures towards disorder and destructiveness within the 'demonized' orders of the world.

This brings our discussion back once again to the story of the flood. As we saw in Genesis 9, God provided an opportunity for a renewed life in a renewed creation. But it was a life of struggle. Part of his loving provision for the fallen world, however, was the restraint of law, and the principle of justice. As we shall see when we come to look at the state in more detail, this covenant made with Noah illustrates a central theme on which Christian social ethics is based: God requires that life be preserved, and the means by which life is preserved, and by which the order necessary for the preservation of life is secured, are the means of justice (verse 6). This theme underlies the civil provisions for order and justice in the Old Testament. This theme, I believe, is presupposed in the Sermon on the Mount.

However, the search for justice in the fallen world is itself a conflict with evil, a weighing of competing claims. It is a recognition that sometimes sin has so trapped us that there are no ways open to us which are good, or that the quest for justice in the face of evil has no option but to use means which themselves incur guilt. We will need to be alert to the fact that moral decision-making in a fallen world is a complex weighing of competing moral claims, of exploring ways of handling conflicting moral principles, and of finding ways of establishing justice which are the least morally compromised.

It is in discussion of these difficult matters that Thielicke describes various situations of what he calls 'the ethical borderline'. For example, he speaks of those situations of injustice 'where sin is institutionalized', or where 'one is confronted by an opponent who is known to be bent wholly on the exercise of his power, and who is obviously on the side of evil'.[10] Thielicke discusses, for example, the ethical dilemmas of the underground movements in wartime; the conflicts between life and life, where to save many lives some may have to be sacrificed; the problems of living with an oath of loyalty given to one who proves he is on the side of evil. In the extreme margins of evil injustice at the ethical borderline, may it not be that the Christian is called on even to use methods of confrontation against evil which themselves are to some degree evil, and thus incur a measure of guilt? If, in the covenant made with Noah, man is required to struggle to preserve the order of society in which life and its values may be preserved, and in which men's lives are protected from 'external destruction and internal perversion'[11], may it not be that sometimes this struggle can *only* be carried on by way of severe moral compromise and the incurring of guilt? Thielicke suggests that in the extremities of the borderline – of which, of course, the questions of modern warfare may well be a clear example – the Christian *is* obliged to engage in such a struggle, but that he can do so only under the conviction of God's command, and of God's forgiveness. The German church's dilemmas of how to respond to the evils of Nazism, and whether or not to assassinate Hitler, are clear examples.

To what extent, though, *may* we connive at one evil in order to avert another? To what extent have we no option but to 'get our hands dirty' in the struggle for justice and for order? What are the boundaries of justice beyond which no action is morally permissible? These are some of the questions we will have to hold in mind when we come to explore more fully the moral dilemmas of modern war.

In and through all this uncertainty, however, one fact remains sure. Despite all the disorders of this present aeon, despite its built-in tendency to self-destruction under the sway of death, the sign of the rainbow is given in the story of Noah as a reminder that the ultimate destiny of this world order is in God's hands. God has 'hung up his bow'. There will be no more flood. The covenant between God and 'every living creature' is an everlasting covenant (Gn.9:16). Our task, as we have said before, is to seek 'while the earth remains' to be faithful, in obedience and allegiance, to him.

Notes for chapter seven

[1]W. D. Davies, *The Setting of the Sermon on the Mount* (CUP, 1964), p.93.
[2]*Ibid.*, p.95.   [3]*Ibid.*, p.433f.
[4]T. W. Manson, *Ethics and the Gospel* (SCM, 1960), p.59.
[5]*Ibid.*, p.59.   [6]*Ibid.*, p.51.
[7]D. Hill, *The Gospel of St Matthew* (Oliphants, 1972), p.127.
[8]*Ibid.*, p.129.
[9]J. R. W. Stott, *Christian Counter-Culture* (IVP, 1978), p.114ff.
[10]H. Thielicke, *Theological Ethics*, 1 (English Translation, Eerdmans, 1968), p.578ff.   [11]*Ibid.*, 2, p.587.

8 Our human predicament

We turn now to some more specific theological 'markers' to help us lay our foundations. We begin in this chapter with a discussion of human life, its sanctity and its disorder. In subsequent chapters we will look at the theological meaning of such central themes as order, justice and peace. We will consider that particular provision of God for the fallen world: the state, its nature, and the limits of its authority. We will discuss the limits to be drawn in the coercive use of force. We conclude by placing the whole discussion in the historical context of eschatological ethics: that this is God's world, and Jesus is his coming King.

Human life: its sanctity
Why, we asked, are there wars?

At the personal level the answer might be the statement of the UNESCO charter: 'Wars begin in the minds of men'. There are wars because human beings are warlike. In the next chapter we will look at the nature of human aggressiveness, which is at the personal root of warfare. We will come to that, however, by way of a prior question: What place does humankind have in the purposes of God? This prior question will also lead us into some related themes: the 'sanctity of human life'; the role of 'man the scientist'; the place of 'nationhood' in the lives of men and women; the question of the possession of land. All of these have a bearing on the issues of war.

The place of human life in this world
We begin with a quotation from Sir Bernard Lovell:

Why is the universe expanding so near the critical rate to prevent its collapse? If the universe had begun to expand in the first few minutes after the explosion of its original incredibly dense state by a rate minutely slower than it did, it would have collapsed back again relatively quickly. And if the expansion of the universe had been different only by a tiny fraction one way or the other from its actual rate, human existence would evidently have been impossible.

Our measurements narrowly define one such universe which had to be that particular universe if it was ever to be known and comprehended by an intelligent being.[1]

One corollary of this, as Torrance expresses it, is that this vast universe is the kind it is because it is necessary for the existence of man. '*Somehow man and the universe are bracketted together.*' However we react to Lovell's view, it certainly meshes well with the theological understanding of the creation of the universe by God, within which human life has so central a place. The climax of the opening chapter of the Bible reads: 'Let us make man in our image . . . So God created man in his own image . . . male and female he created them' (Gn.1:26f.). The majestic words of the psalmist underline the theme: 'What is man that thou art mindful of him? . . . Yet thou hast made him little less than God, and dost crown him with glory and honour' (Ps.8:4f.). The New Testament constantly illustrates the true humanity of Jesus as the 'first-born' of all creation in whom all things hold together (Col.1:15ff.). These themes all underline the exceptional place of human life in the purposes of God. Jesus Christ himself is 'perfect God and perfect man' united into one 'not by conversion of the Godhead into flesh, but by taking of the manhood into God' (Athanasian Creed). Here is a picture of humankind as the crown and climax of God's creative work. We should not be surprised, therefore, to discover that biblical authors stress that human life is precious.

The sanctity of human life
Christians have often spoken of 'the sanctity of human life'. What does this phrase mean? The word 'sanctity' points to the notion of 'holiness', a word used primarily of God himself, and then also of the 'sacredness' of those 'separated' or

dedicated to God. The 'sanctity of human life' thus refers to a 'holiness by association' with God. Because of this, Christians affirm, human life is to be respected and normally to be protected.

One of the biblical themes which points towards this understanding of life's sanctity is that human beings are made 'in the image of God'. There has been a great deal written on the meaning of 'the image of God'. A reference from the New Testament will help point us in the right direction. Paul speaks of the 'image of God' using the analogy of a mirror, and then referring to the person of Jesus Christ. 'We all . . . beholding (literally 'as in a mirror') the glory of the Lord are being changed into his likeness.' A little later he speaks of 'the glory of Christ, who is the likeness of God' (2 Cor.3:18; 4:4). Christ, in other words, reflects the image of God as a mirror reflects the image of the object which we see 'in' the mirror. And all of us Christians are gradually being changed so as to reflect that image more fully. Now for us to see an image in a mirror, the mirror's *relationship* to the object is all-important. So for Christ to be 'in the image of God' means that he is in a particular relationship to God. So part of what it means to speak of human beings 'in the image of God' is to express our special relationship to him in the created order. However, whereas Christ is perfect and mirrors God perfectly, God's image in the rest of us is to a great extent distorted and out of line. But, despite the distortion, God has called us to a special relationship with himself, in which something of his divine nature is to be seen.

There is a second aspect also. As both the Genesis creation text and Psalm 8, for example, make clear, human beings are to *represent and mediate God's rule* in the world: to 'have dominion over' other creatures. The 'image' is thus a *task* as well as a relationship. Both the relationship and the task set human life apart from every other form of created life. Human life is special, not because of human achievements, but because God has declared that this particular species will express his image, to reflect something of his nature and to care for his world.

Alongside the theological description of man made 'in the image of God', other biblical themes also lend support to the notion of the sacredness of human life. First, human life is pictured as God's *gift*. When Ruth married Boaz, and he went in to her and she bore a son (Ru.4:13), we read of God's involvement in the processes of life in these words: 'the Lord gave her conception'. This notion of life as God's gift underlies other biblical allusions to life before birth (*cf.* Je.1:5; Ps.139; Lk.1; *etc.*). The way some of the psalmists refer to God's 'sustaining' of human life (*e.g.* Ps.104:27f.) points in the same direction. Life from its earliest beginnings is God's gift. Karl Barth changes the picture by referring to life not so much as a gift but more as a *loan* from God, a thought which suggests the stewardship of life held on trust from God, to whom we are answerable.

Secondly, another biblical theme which supports the notion of the 'sanctity of human life' is – as some of the Psalms to which we have already referred make clear – that human beings are persons *known by God*:

> For thou didst form my inward parts, thou didst knit me together in my mother's womb.
> I praise thee, for thou art fearful and wonderful. Wonderful are thy works! Thou knowest me right well;
> my frame was not hidden from thee, when I was being made in secret, intricately wrought in the depths of the earth.
> Thy eyes beheld my unformed substance; in thy book were written, every one of them, the days that were formed for me, when as yet there was none of them.
> How precious to me are thy thoughts, O God! How vast is the sum of them! (Ps.139:13–17).

If human life, then, is created in the divine image, is a gift – or a loan – from God's hand, is personal life in which each person is known by God himself, then human life is to be respected and protected. There is a 'sanctity' to human life.

That is not to say that sanctity is an *absolute* sanctity. The Old Testament makes clear in a number of places that belief in life as God's gift can be held together with the acceptance of capital punishment for a number of crimes (*e.g.* Gn.9:6; Ex.21:15f.; 21:23; Dt.22:21, 22, 24, 25; 24:16; *etc.*). However, 'the principle, properly used, asserts a human right to enjoy protection in life and bodily integrity; that right may be violated only for just cause approved by the general moral sense and by public authority'.[2]

No shedding of innocent blood
One of the ways in which the Old Testament upheld the sanctity of human life was its insistence on forbidding the shedding of innocent blood. After the deluge of the flood, the story of God's blessing of Noah includes an insistence on the sacredness of life, and a ban on murder. Blood in the Scriptures is a symbol of life, and it is precisely to preserve the sanctity of life that the command for capital punishment is appropriate to the covenant made with Noah in Genesis 9:6: 'Whoever sheds the blood of man, by man shall his blood be shed'. The Decalogue also makes the law explicit: '"Thou shalt do no murder."' Blood which is shed defiles the land in which Yahweh dwells, and must be expiated by the blood of him who shed it (Nu.35:31–34). It was to protect life and the conditions necessary for life, as we saw in the Old Testament wars of conquest, that God sometimes commanded war. It was to protect life that the 'cities of refuge' were provided for those who killed another unintentionally (Dt.19:4ff.). Other shedding of innocent blood was dealt with by the 'blood vengeance' (*e.g.* 2 Sa.3:22–27, 30), a most solemn responsibility of the next of kin, and the best way a desert community could give expression to the faith that a just God called them to practise justice. Gradually, of course, the institution of judicial family killing of those who shed innocent blood was replaced by the growing power of the state.

In the prophets we find reference to the heinous crime of shedding innocent blood (Is.59:7; Je.22:3,17; Ezk.22:4; *etc.*); and the New Testament also speaks in strong terms against those whose 'feet are swift to shed blood' (Rom.3:15 quoting Is.59:7). It reminds us that Judas' conviction of sin was in 'betraying innocent blood' (Mt.27:4). Human life was to be respected and protected because it was precious. Innocent blood should not be shed, and precautions had to be taken to prevent it.

While, therefore, we cannot argue from the Old or New Testament that the 'sanctity of human life' is an absolute principle such that no life must ever be taken, it does seem clear that to take the life of an 'innocent' person is seen as a severe crime and sin before God.

When we try to apply this to the taking of life in warfare, it is of course – especially in the modern world – difficult to use the term 'innocent' in the way the term is used in the Bible. However, as we shall see, the important distinction in 'just war' theory between combatants and non-combatants, and the crucial criterion of non-combatant immunity, are ways of trying to give expression to this principle. (It is of particular note that Karl Barth chooses to discuss the ethics of war in a section of his *Church Dogmatics* headed 'Respect for Life'.) Our thinking about war needs to begin with the preciousness of human life which is normally to be protected.

Man the scientist

It is appropriate at this point to comment briefly on another implication of the 'task' given to humankind made 'in the image of God', namely the creation mandate to 'have dominion over' and subdue the rest of creation. Man was given the task of controlling and using the natural order for God's glory and for the benefit of his world. This involved discovering its secrets and bringing to articulation its hidden order. Man the scientist is to be steward of God's world, discovering its truth and using that truth in technological care of creation for God's sake and the blessing of his creation.

The destiny of humankind is bound up with its calling and responsibility to be steward of God's creation. This is how many of the early scientists who were Christians perceived their task: to think God's thoughts after him. How far this seems from the 'military-industrial complex'! How far from much of today's technology which too often operates in terms not of a quest for truth, but of a cost-benefit manipulation of truth for the sake of other goals dictated by economic, utilitarian or political pressures. How many of today's creative minds are necessarily employed on 'defence', and the development of ever more sophisticated means of mass destruction, whether for aggression or for deterrence. They are employed, in other words, in work, the sensitivity of which means that there is little chance for really creative risk-taking in the development of new science. We do well to remember technological man at the Tower of Babel, who ended in confusion and isolation (described as expressions of divine judgment) through trying to build in contempt of the truth.

In today's world where so much science and technology is being directed towards weapons of destruction and ecological devastation, we need again to learn how to place our science within the constraints of a God-given moral universe, and ask whether our technological expertise is being used to further the task of conservation and stewardship, or is in fact frustrating that God-given responsibility.

One of the other factors which dominate the life of Western man is the acceptance of economic growth alongside technological advance as the ultimate social good. The economic sphere is coming to dominate every other aspect of life. We are being guided not by the norm of stewardship but by the goal of increasing production. We are failing to allow economic and technological factors to be open to evaluation in the light of other moral and spiritual dimensions to life. When this is coupled with the fact that the present economic world system operates on the basis of a 'core' of wealth dominating a 'periphery' of poverty, we see the force of Wolterstorff's comment that our practice of treating economic growth as an autonomous and ultimate good is nothing but idolatry.[3]

Our concern for the preciousness of human life and for the creative and stewardly tasks given to mankind by God means that we cannot ignore the structures and systems of political and economic life which create injustice and feed a sense of economic domination and oppression. It is in such soil that seeds of violence and war tend to grow.

Humanity and nationality

Man, created male and female in the divine image, was created also for community. The Old Testament emphasis on corporate solidarity and the New Testament metaphors of the Body of Christ alike remind us that the nature of man is not to be understood *first* as an individual and *then* as a member of society, but by seeing his functions and relationships as a totality. Men and women are created for personal relationships. Personal communion between people, the fellowship of community, is partly what the image of God is about, derived as it is from the communion between the Father and the Son in the Godhead in the fellowship of the Spirit.

The seeds of war are often nurtured by an ideological commitment to certain sorts of community obligations: to national sovereignty, national honour and national survival, which can be held to the exclusion of any notion of common humanity under God. How are we to think of nationhood from a theological perspective?

The covenant theme of both Old and New Testaments points to the fact that God works by families. It is from him that every family in heaven and on earth receives its name (Eph.3:15). We belong to others. We need one another. In all the variety of our personal, sexual, racial, cultural and national diversities, we are part of a single humanity made for fellowship.

It is only after this affirmation of our common humanity has been stressed that the rightness of national divisions and cultural diversity can be assessed. It is clear that the Old

Testament focuses on one chosen nation to whom Messiah came, and through whom light would shine to lighten the Gentiles (Is.42:6; 49:6). The Christian church is seen in the New Testament as a new, multinational community, a 'holy nation' (1 Pet.2:9). Whatever our sex, social status or earthly nationality (Jew or Greek, male or female, slave or free: Gal.3:28), we are 'one in Christ Jesus'. The 'blessing of Abraham' has now come upon the nations (Gal.3:14). Yet, as O. R. Johnston notes in his *Nationhood*[4], the children of God through faith still bear the marks of different cultures, still retain sexual and related personality distinctions, still exist in given communities with particular social structures. Grace does not abolish these. So in the providence of God, national diversity within the unity of humankind is assumed in the biblical writings, and 'there is no indication that the diversity of nations will be or ought to be replaced by any unified international order in which nationhood is absorbed'. Johnston quotes Solzhenitsyn's Nobel lecture:

> The disappearance of nations would impoverish us no less than if all the people were made alike, with one character, one face. Nations are the wealth of mankind, they are its generalized personalities; the smallest of them has its own particular colours and embodies a particular facet of God's design.[6]

Indeed, the picture of Revelation 13 suggests that if and when world government does emerge, it could be the most monstrous force for inhumanity and persecution that history has seen.

There does, then, seem to be a positive acceptance of national identity and cultural diversity in Scripture. Nationhood is part of the richness of God's providential ordering of his world. But nationhood is not an absolute. When nationhood becomes an absolute principle, it becomes demonic. As Johnston points out, following Barth, 'nationhood' is not an 'order of creation' – we must not obliterate the distinction between divine command and divine providence. National life is to be cherished and sustained, but not absolutized. National honour is to be affirmed as one colour in the spectrum of the richness of human diversity, not to be asserted at the expense of our common humanity. When a nation considers *itself* sovereign rather than in submission to the sovereign Lord, and when pride in national membership supercedes all other identifications, then 'Legitimate nationalism has . . . become idolatrous nationalism. . . . For the signs of nationalism gone cancerous the Christian, and everyone else, must be constantly alert . . . there is nothing more destructive of shalom than such nationalism.'[7]

Man and territory

How many modern wars are concerned essentially about land, or about the valuable natural resources which the land holds? What does Christian theology say about land? Again, the Old Testament will give us our lead in.

It is not only respect for life, individual, communal and national, which the Christian doctrine of creation requires, but also respect for the earth and the environment in which human life is to be lived. 'The earth is the LORD's', sings the psalmist. And the writer of Genesis 2:15 speaks of man's calling to care for God's garden. As von Rad comments: 'this verse . . . indicates man's purpose in being in the garden: he is to work it and preserve it from all damage . . . work was man's sober destiny even in his original state. That man was transferred to the garden to guard it indicates that he was called to a state of service and had to prove himself in a realm that was not his own possession.'[8]

Land, therefore, is seen in the Old Testament as being entrusted to man as God's vicegerent. But God is the Lord of the soil. The land which the Lord gives to his people, land which had been promised to their fathers, is still 'the LORD's land' (Jos.22:19; *cf*. Ps.85:1). The 'property-right' which God retained over all the land was the basis on which the law of the Jubilee was founded (Lv.25:23): '"The land shall not be sold in perpetuity, for the land is mine; for you are strangers and sojourners with me."'

Humankind will be held accountable for the stewardship they have given of God's property. Before there is any talk about personal 'property-rights', or national sovereign territory, or even individual possessions – appropriate as these may be in their place – the first conviction that needs to be re-emphasized is that 'the earth is the LORD's', and the human task is primarily one of stewardship.

Human life: its destructiveness

If, in the Creator's purpose, man – male and female – is made in God's image to reflect his character, to share his fellowship and to care for his world, this purpose is far from evident in the way human beings behave and in the disorder their lives display. Christian theology speaks not only of creation, but also of fall.

When the UNESCO Charter declared 'Wars begin in the minds of men', it was concerned not so much with the psychological disposition of human beings which drives people to mutual destruction, but with the lack of knowledge of the other person which needs to be made good by education. 'What makes men fight each other is their failure to perceive their common nature or interest', comments Booth[9]. However, it is an oversimplification to imagine that the spread of information, the breaking down of caricatures, the development of cultural exchanges – important though these are – will reduce man's innate aggressiveness. The psychological and spiritual dimensions must not be minimized.

We noted in our glance at the New Testament in Chapter 2, how the Epistle of James sums up the causes of war in terms of 'human passions'. In theological terms, the aggressiveness of human beings can be traced back to sin in the heart of man. The story of the fall in Genesis 3 indicates the way in which disorder in a person's relationship with God leads to disruption in his relationships with himself, with others, with his environment. The continuation of that story in the narrative of Cain and Abel in Genesis 4 illustrates how such sin can lead to jealousy and hence to aggressiveness between fellow human beings. The Genesis narrative illustrates the progression from Cain and Abel to the wickedness described in the story of Noah, to the Tower of Babel, to the aggressiveness of the Sodom story, and so on. There is something about fallen human nature which tends towards aggressive cruelty and destructiveness.

Psychologist Erich Fromm comes to precisely the same conclusion from a completely different starting point. In *The Anatomy of Human Destructiveness* he distinguishes between two entirely different kinds of aggression in a person. The first, which he shares with all animals, is a genetically programmed impulse to attack (or to flee) when vital interests are threatened. This *defensive*, 'benign' aggression is in the service of the survival of the individual and of the species, is biologically adaptive, and ceases when the threat has ceased to exist. The other type, 'malignant' aggression, is specific to the human species, and virtually absent in most mammals. It has no purpose, and its satisfaction is lustful.

Defensive aggression as seen in all the animal world, Fromm argues, is part of human nature. However, 'man differs from the animal by the fact that he is a killer; he is the only primate that kills and tortures members of his own species without any reason, either biological or economic, and who feels satisfaction in doing so'.[10] Fromm then goes on to say that while it may be right to understand the one sort of aggression in terms of instincts which answer to man's physiological needs, the other derives from specifically human passions rooted in man's character. Is he by nature driven by love and creativity, or by the passion to destroy? Fromm's own analysis leans heavily on Freudian psychoanalytic theory and develops into an optimistic form of humanism with which orthodox Christian faith would have difficulty. But his understanding of human aggressiveness, as we have outlined it, agrees with that given centuries earlier by the Epistle of James.

We need, therefore, an understanding of the nature of humankind which guards against too facile a description. The predominant view of the biblical authors does not follow the eventual optimism of Fromm nor, for example, that of Rousseau who believed that 'man is naturally good, and only by institutions is he made bad. ... To undo evil, it is only necessary to abandon civilisation, for man is naturally good, and savage man, when he has dined, is at peace with all nature and the friend of all his fellow creatures.'[11] Neither, on the other hand, do the biblical authors endorse a pessimism of human nature, such as we find in the empiricist philosopher Thomas Hobbes: 'In a state of nature, before there is any government, every man desires to preserve his own liberty, and also to acquire dominion over others. Both these desires are dictated by the impulse to self-preservation. From their conflict arises a war of all against all, which makes life solitary, poor, nasty, brutish and short.'[12]

The predominant view of man presented by the biblical authors is of the ambiguity of human nature, with all the richness which flows from being made in the image of God, and all the disorder which results from man's disorientation in relationship with his Creator. There is on the one hand, a proper creative assertiveness in being human, implied in the command to 'have dominion over' the rest of the created order. Any human achievement requires some degree of assertiveness. As Anthony Storr[13] illustrates, it has found its way into the language of achievement: we *attack* problems, we *get our teeth into* them, we *master* a subject when we have *struggled with* and *overcome* its difficulties. We *sharpen* our wits and so on. *But* on the other hand this proper sense of assertiveness easily slips over into a cruel and destructive aggressiveness which attempts to exercise dominion over my fellow for my own benefit. To quote Storr again:

It is a tragic paradox that the very qualities which have led to man's extraordinary success are also most likely to destroy him. His ruthless drive to subdue or destroy every apparent obstacle in his path does not stop short of his own fellows; and since he now possesses weapons of unparallelled destructiveness and also apparently lacks the built-in safeguards which prevent most animals from killing others of the same species, it is not beyond possibility that he may yet encompass the total elimination of *homo sapiens*.[14]

This 'tragic paradox' Christian theology interprets in terms of the fallenness of mankind from the Creator's will.

A theological realism, then, must deal seriously with man's sin. And this is crucially important in coming to a Christian assessment of war.

Power

One of the aspects of human life which illustrates further the ambiguity of human nature is the exercise of power. Power can be analysed at one level in terms of a psychological impulse (what Nietzsche and others have called a 'will to power') which drives a person to control and dominate others; or at another level in terms of its purpose as the capacity to achieve a desired goal. Either way, we find in practice an ambiguity related to that of our human nature.

There can, of course, be a right exercise of power. God is a 'God of power and might' whose power is seen in his creativity, his dominion over his creation, his sovereign purposes for his world. Yet his power is only exercised as an expression of his character of holy love. In human relationships – all of which have an element of power – there can likewise be a right use of God-given creativity, 'dominion' and striving for God's purposes in the world. And – as in appropriate family discipline – coercive power can be used by one human being over another as an expression of parental love.

However, the fallenness of our nature accounts for the other readily observed feature of the human exercise of power, namely that in practice there is a bias towards a fundamentally self-interested and potentially destructive use of power. In particular, the concentrations of power in human groups whose primary concern or unconscious task is their own survival, leads to a tendency to use power in a destructively aggressive way.

This fact has led in practice to the political necessity to limit power by institutional safeguards. The constitutional pattern used to limit human power, and prevent its destructive mis-use, is usually called 'the distribution of powers'. This, as Thielicke notes, is 'an institutional expression of an abiding mistrust of power, or rather of people in power. The call for a distribution of powers is a partly conscious and partly unconscious recognition of the reality of the fall and the unreliability of fallen man.'[15]

In a later section we will examine more fully the appropriate uses of coercive force, and the relationship between power and love.

Christian realism

The Christian realist, trying to be true to his understanding of the nature of man as created, and yet as fallen, will refuse to approach the question of war either in terms of despairing fatalism, or in terms of utopian optimism. While everything possible must be done to avert them, he will acknowledge with sadness that until the Lord comes there will be 'wars and rumours of wars' (Mk.13:7). He will not be so naïvely idealistic as to say 'if only . . . then there would be no more war', because his understanding of sin tells him that human nature is not changed by treaty or conference. Human wickedness cannot be negotiated away. Furthermore, to take seriously the deceitfulness of sin should alert him to the folly of placing too much reliance on the infallible rationality of those in power. And that is especially significant in our assessment of certain aspects of deterrence policy. For while deterrence on the one hand can tend to foster a sense of mistrust and even of fatalism, on the other hand it assumes that men are essentially rational and reliable. Christian theology puts both emphases the other way round: we are not in the grip of an inevitable fate – we are responsible for the choices we make, and our choices are significant; but in all our choosing there is a tendency to self-interest, irrationality and deceit.

While the Christian holds the vision of the coming time when the victory of Christ over evil will be complete, and when, as the prophets said, swords will be beaten into ploughshares and spears into pruning hooks, he knows that there will be no utopia this side of heaven. What are needed, then, are social structures which provide a context of order and justice in which precious human life may be preserved and protected, and in which human creativity in the stewardship of God's world can flourish. What are needed also are ways of restraining man's powerful tendencies to destructiveness. We need structures which can contain man's tendency to be warlike, communications systems which maximize trust and minimize opportunities for deceit, and patterns of social order with such built-in checks and balances that human power is distributed and separated.

We shall see that one God-given provision for establishing such structures and restraints is the institution of the state, but, as we shall also see, a state with particular authority, particular goals and particular limits. Before we look more fully at the state, however, we need first to ask in more detail what is meant by 'order' and what is meant by 'justice'. From these discussions we will then be in a position to explore a theological understanding of the meaning of 'peace'.

Notes for chapter eight

[1]Sir Bernard Lovell quoted in T. F. Torrance, *The Ground and Grammar of Theology* (Christian Journals Ltd, 1980), p.3.

[2]G. R. Dunstan in A. S. Duncan, G. R. Dunstan & R. B. Welbourn (eds.), *Dictionary of Medical Ethics*, 2nd ed. (DLT, 1981), p.384.

[3]N. Wolterstorff, *Until Justice and Peace Embrace* (Eerdmans, 1983), p.66.

[4]O. R. Johnston, *Nationhood* (Latimer Studies, 1980), *passim*.   [5]*Ibid.*

[6]A. Solzhenitsyn, *One Word of Truth* (Nobel Prize Lecture, 1971), pp.15f., in O. R. Johnston, *ibid.*, p.18.

[7]Wolterstorff, *op.cit.*, p.109.

[8]G. von Rad, *Genesis* (English Translation, SCM, 1961), p.78.

[9] A. Booth, *Not Only Peace* (SCM, 1967), p.17.

[10] E. Fromm, *The Anatomy of Human Destructiveness* (Penguin ed., 1977), p.25.

[11] J. J. Rousseau, *Discourse on Inequality* (1754), p.11, in B. Russell, *History of Western Philosophy* (Allen & Unwin, 1946), p.663.

[12] T. Hobbes, *Leviathan* Part I ch.13, M. Oakeshott (ed.), (Blackwells, 1946), p.82.

[13] A. Storr, *Human Aggression* (Penguin, 1968).

[14] *Ibid.*, p.12.

[15] H. Thielicke, *Theological Ethics*, **2** (English Translation, Eerdmans, 1969), p.210.

9 Order, justice and peace

Introduction

The state, as we have hinted and will argue more fully later, is intended to meet the need for justice to be established, and this requires a system of social order. But the order and justice for which the state is responsible are not arbitrary creations of government: they are, as we shall see, rooted in morality. The state's concern is for order, but 'order' must be defined by a more ultimate order derived from the nature of God himself. The state's concern is justice, but justice, too, needs to be defined by reference to the justice of God. How to understand these terms theologically is our task in this next chapter. When we have explored these questions we will be in a position to ask: 'What, then, is peace?'

God's order and ours

There are two strands of Old Testament thought, brought together in much of the New Testament material, from which our thinking about God's 'order' must begin: belief in creation and the notion of wisdom.

The striking feature of the first creation account in Genesis 1 is the beautiful order of God's world from which, the writer believes, an ordered pattern of a seven-day week is derived. The ordering of this particular pattern of human life is congruent with the divine order of creation itself. Behind the order and chaos of this present world, in other words, there is a divine order which is to some degree disclosed in the patterns of the created world. This, indeed, is one of the essential presuppositions of the scientific enterprise. There could be no science, and no technology, were there not sufficient grounds for the assumption of rationality, predictability and coherence in the universe on which to base the scientific enterprise.

That there is a moral component to the divine ordering of the world is disclosed through the revelation of God, especially in the early days of Israel through the Law and the Prophets. The moral prescriptions of God's law in the Torah are not arbitrary commands: they derive from and are expressions of the moral character of God himself, and therefore of the moral fabric of the universe. On this foundation, a moral pattern of life appropriate for people made in God's image is given: hence the detailed prescriptions of laws relating to human living. Perhaps the clearest example of the way the order of the divine nature is applied to patterns of human conduct may be seen in the Holiness Code. In Leviticus 19 all the various aspects of human life: domestic, religious, cultic, social, economic, personal, agricultural and so on, are regulated by rules which apply the divine nature: 'I am the LORD' (verses 4, 10, 12, 14, 16, 18, 25, 28, 30, 31, 32, 34, 37; cf. verse 2). It is because of the nature of God the Creator that there is a pattern of life appropriate for his creatures.

It is God's order for the world to which the literature of the wisdom tradition also points. Wisdom is that style of writing, and the approach to life which it carries, which we find in books like Proverbs, Job and Ecclesiastes. They offer guidance in 'coping' with living in the ambiguities of this fallen world. These books observe life; they search for patterns in the world and in events. There is also an underlying conviction that the patterns of the world must rest on some deeper hidden order, derived only from God. As the book of Job shows, humanist wisdom which creates its own patterns can give no rest for the soul. But 'if a man rigorously pursues that openness to facts which is humanism's characteristic boast, he will find either that his confidence disintegrates and he is thrown into despairing scepticism, or that he is brought to a faith in which his discernment of order in human existence is discovered to have its explanation in the being of a personal God'.[1] Such is the conviction of the wisdom writers.

The same conviction of a divine order discernible to some degree by men underlies much of the New Testament. Just as God makes his rain to fall on the evil as well as the good, so Christ's disciples must love their enemies as well as their friends, so that they may be seen to follow the pattern of their Father who is in heaven (*cf.* Mt.5:45ff.). Here is a sort of 'natural law'. Jesus points also to those who 'know how to give good gifts to their children': there is an unquestioned acceptance of something which is 'good'. In Jesus' discussion of divorce, he appeals not only to the Law but also to the patterns of creation (Mt.19:3f.). The way we are made, and reflection on what makes for the best for us, both point to an underlying belief that we are living in a world which is ordered and moral, and derived from the hands of God.

Perhaps this is the sort of thinking which lies behind the two classic passages in Paul which also indicate the existence of some sort of 'natural law' within the human consciousness, related to the patterns of God's created order (Rom.1:19–21; 2:14–15). People can distinguish good from evil because they are human; that is, in their very make-up they do – whether they acknowledge it or not – reflect the divine image.

When we come to a discussion of the state, therefore, we shall need to remind ourselves that its concern for order is no arbitrary human construction. The state exists within a moral order derived from God. Its own existence and its prescriptions for human living are to be seen in the light of the moral boundaries of God's character and his will for human life. The state, in other words, is not beyond morality. Nor is it beyond the sphere of moral criticism.

Whereas it may well be that the state may do what an individual may not do, both operate within the same moral universe and are accountable to the same moral God.

God's justice and ours

What do we mean when we speak of 'justice'? Calvin spoke of a universal concern among men that they and others ought to live justly: 'there exist in all men's minds universal impressions of a certain civic fair dealing and order'[2]. In ordinary human speech, justice is about 'rights' – the legitimate claim which one person exercises on another or others for fair dealing. When we say that a person is 'just' we mean that he acts in a way which respects others' rights. Justice in this ordinary sense is about the minimum required for a society to live in the sort of order which respects rights.

Many people divide justice into 'contractual' justice: the right to receive what is expected from someone with whom a contract has been made; 'distributive justice': the relative rights of individuals to share in the society of which they are part; and 'retributive justice', which refers to the relationship between offenders against the law and those responsible for the upholding of law. To what extent the state should primarily be concerned with 'law and order' in the negative sense of 'punishing evildoers', and to what extent it should be primarily concerned with the 'benefit rights' of an equitable distribution of available resources, is part of the spectrum of political disagreement. But 'justice' in common speech refers to both: to rights and to obligations. It concerns the social framework in which individuals seek to exercise their rights.

Lewis Smedes' book *Mere Morality*[3] is an exposition of the Decalogue in terms of those human rights which he suggests justice requires us to uphold. The command to worship indicates a 'right' to assemble for worship without interference; the command against stealing indicates a right to possess what is one's own; the command against adultery points to a right to fidelity from one's spouse; the command against murder underlines the right to life. We might add that the incentives towards stewardship implicit in the command to work indicate a right to a share in the earth's resources.

Justice is not served merely by affirming rights, however, but when rights are actually upheld. It is part of the function of the state to bear responsibility for distributive justice in our society. And not only within our own society: we are part of the human family made of one blood (Acts 17:26). We need to call in question any view which suggests that a person's share in the earth's resources should be determined by the place of his birth.

Furthermore, there are basic *sustenance* rights which we have as human beings. But our share in the resources available to sustain life are in large measure related to the social and economic structures by which this world system operates. This points us again to the way in which social structures can have an effect on human flourishing. 'We have a claim on our fellow human beings to social arrangements that ensure that we will be adequately sustained in existence.'[4]

It is in the actual political decisions concerning the establishment of justice in a world of competing claims and deep-seated self-interest that we often find the seeds of war. The pressing issues of world hunger and world energy needs and resources, which are likely to promote increasingly the instability that erupts into war, are priorities for Christians called to find ways of establishing justice.

The justice of God

But how does what we have just seen tie in with the biblical notion of the justice of God? He is proclaimed as the one who 'executes justice' (Dt.10:17–18). And, though often expressed by other words (such as 'judgments' or 'righteousness'), the Bible is full of the language of justice.

God's justice means several things.

The term refers first to the will and character of God. 'The Rock, his work is perfect; for all his ways are justice. A God of faithfulness and without iniquity, just and right is he'

130

(Dt.32:4). God's justice is then used as the standard by which he measures human conduct. 'What does the LORD require of you but to do justice, and to love kindness, and to walk humbly with your God?' (Mi.6:8). Justice is used of the appropriate punishment for sin ('the due reward for our deeds', Lk.23:41), and also as the vindication of good and right behaviour. It is in this sense of *vindication* that some of the strands of Old Testament thought see the justice of God in the victory of war. The Psalmist writes: 'O sing to the LORD a new song, for he has done marvellous things! His right hand and his holy arm have gotten him victory. The LORD has made known his victory, he has revealed his vindication in the sight of the nations' (Ps.98:1–2).

With God, however, justice gives more than ordinary human justice requires. Divine justice merges into love and grace. Divine justice *becomes redemptive*. Much of the Old Testament reminds us how God *in justice* acts *to redeem* his people (and so in a sense *vindicates* them). Many Psalms pick up the theme. Isaiah speaks of 'a righteous God and [therefore] a Saviour' (Is.45:21).

The qualities of justice (*mishpat*), righteousness (*tsedeq*) and mercy (*chesed*) are, though at first sight distinguishable in meaning, never separable in fact in God's actions towards us. His justice is permeated by his righteousness and his mercy.[5] The New Testament speaks of his faithfulness and justice precisely in his forgiveness (1 Jn.1:9) and his grace (*cf.* the parable of the labourers, Mt.20:15).

Most clearly of all, punitive and redemptive justice come together in the cross of Christ. As Paul says, 'he himself is righteous and ... justifies him who has faith in Jesus' (Rom.3:26); he 'justifies the ungodly' (Rom.4:5) precisely because he 'is righteous' (Rom.3:26). Both punishment and grace meet in the death of Christ (Rom.3:25). God's holy and just moral nature is most characteristically expressed in the justice which includes forgiveness, and in the grace which goes beyond the mere demands of the law.

One of the strong emphases in the Old Testament, which is

carried over also into the New, is that God's justice is seen in particular in his passion for the needs of the poor and the oppressed. Widows are often singled out for particular legal protection (Dt.10:17–18). The prophets make much of the rights of the poor and needy (*e.g.* Is.10:1–2; Am.5:12). The Messianic King will deliver the oppressed (Ps.72:1–4; Is.9:7). The New Testament picks up this theme. The day will come when the inequities of human justice are reversed, when the mighty are put down from their thrones, and those of low degree are exalted (Lk.1:52).

The New Testament also reminds us that it is in God's new heaven and new earth that 'righteousness dwells' (2 Pet.3:13). In that Day, the wrath of God will be revealed as his 'righteous judgment' against evil (Rom.2:5), and fire will test 'what sort of work' each has done (1 Cor.3:13).

It is within such a context of the justice of God that human justice is to be expressed. God's justice begins in his moral character which defines good and separates good from evil, thus providing the basis for punishment; it moves into the concern for the establishment of justice in dealings between people, with a special concern for those who are oppressed; it merges into grace and mercy with its characteristic note of forgiveness; it points towards the new world in which 'righteousness dwells'. In our human relationships we are called to express something of this aspect of the divine character. Paul says as much in 2 Corinthians 8 and 9. He reminds his readers of God's concern for the poor, and calls on them to share their financial resources 'that there may be equality'. And why? Because this is the way the grace of God has come to us in Christ. Our justice in Christian affairs must correspond with God's, and can do so because God works through us in grace.

Karl Barth summarizes this so well:

The human righteousness required by God and established in obedience, the righteousness which according to Amos 5:24 should pour down as a mighty stream – has necessarily the character of a vindication of right in favour of the threatened innocent, the oppressed poor, widows, orphans and aliens. For this reason, in the relations and events in the life of His people, God always takes His stand unconditionally and passionately on this side and on this side alone: against the lofty and on behalf of the lowly; against those who already enjoy right and privilege and on behalf of those who are denied and deprived of it.[6]

The relation between God's justice and ours

So what is the relation between God's justice and ours? In Paul Ramsey's phrase: biblical justice 'transforms' human justice. All human efforts after justice are beset by human sinfulness, but the biblical picture of the meaning of justice both sets standards by which human behaviour is to be measure, and holds out a motivation for seeking to move nearer to justice in human society. Justice will never be fully realized until Messiah's kingdom is fully established. However, it remains a biblical promise and hope. Although we cannot establish perfect justice this side of heaven, we can and should move towards it. As Paul wrote to the Philippians, it is an essential Christian concern that we look not only to our own interests, but also to 'the interests of others' (Phil.2:4). While Christians must seek more than bare 'human' justice, we can never seek less.

What does this amount to in the context of war?

If justice is about the vindication of right, expressed in a manner that is touched with forgiveness and mercy, we can see that, while justice may sometimes need enforcing against unjust structures or aggressive evil, measured by God's redemptive and merciful justice our human quest for the justice of some wars and for justice in war can only ever be undertaken under the rubric of penitence and divine mercy.

In a poignant section of a Remembrance Day sermon, Oliver O'Donovan referred to the Psalmist's call for a new

133

song because of the Lord's vindication in the sight of the nations:

> Victory as vindication! In that combination of ideas lies the seed of how war has been thought of by Christendom. It is an arbitration of right. And in that arbitration we may hope to see disclosed God's own vindication of justice. When we do see it, we should sing unto the Lord a new song, glad, not for ourselves alone, but for our enemies and for all mankind. For God's vindication of justice is the promise of the possibility of life. It is his bow in the clouds, his covenant that men will not be swallowed by the flood.

But then he goes on:

> If we are at all sensitive we will shudder at the boldness of this claim. For we see very much in war besides the vindication of justice. We see monstrous wrong done – and not only by the party that is apparently *in* the wrong; but sometimes we see the worst done by those who have the best reason to think their cause just. To think of war in terms of justice, then, exposes us not only to gladness but to self-critical penitence. It forces us to acknowledge all that has made us poor instruments of justice – the anger, the intolerance, the impatience, and the partisan perspective into which even our just causes may have betrayed us. . . .[7]

Justice, forgiveness, and the need to be forgiven. Can our politics hold these together?

Just means
One further question has to be raised at this point: May justice only be vindicated by just means, or may just ends sometimes be used to justify means that are themselves unjust? In what Thielicke called 'the ethical borderline' we may sometimes be confronted with situations in which no

way open is good, and there is no apparent objective weighting available to us for evaluating the lesser evil of the options
that are open. Can we act unjustly then, for the sake of a just
goal? Thielicke's examples are of the extreme situations of
the willingness to betray some colleagues in a concentration
camp, for the sake of the release of many more; or of the
willingness to use torture to gain information essential to the
safety of many. Can unjust means in such cases be justified?

Even there, we are not – as Thielicke himself makes clear –
permitted to ignore the means used to achieve a desired end.
The use of immoral means for the sake of a moral end may,
in fact, alter and destroy the very end it was intended to
attain.[8] Thielicke illustrates this in part by reference to the
temptations of Jesus (Mt.4:1–11). By using the means of
earthly power granted him by the devil, it would seem that
Jesus could have quickly ushered in the kingdom of God on
earth. And yet, if he had chosen that way, instead of the way
of lowly suffering, obedience to God, taking the form of the
servant, the kingdom Jesus would have inaugurated would
itself have been a 'mere caricature' of the truth. The kingdom would not have been what it is in truth, a concealed
object of faith, and a pattern of life under God's rule, marked
by obedient service. It would have been its opposite: a public
and visible earthly kingdom built on coercive earthly force.

Likewise, the Christian task of establishing justice cannot
be achieved by means that are themselves unjust, or else the
goal which is achieved may in fact be its opposite. The 'just
war' theories were right to give as one of their criteria *jus in
bello* – there must be *just means* in the waging of war. Justice is
not served by using injustice. We will need to come back to
this question again, particularly in our discussion of modern
weapons of indiscriminate destructiveness.

Justice and love
The moral character of God which orders the world; the
righteous dealing of God which vindicates justice and gra-
ciously forgives; these are different parts of what is involved

in saying 'God is love'. What, then, is the relation between 'love' (especially when we read the command to love our enemies) and 'justice'?

Paul Ramsey put it this way[9]: Love, he says, regards the good of the other as more important than your own good, when only you and he are involved; but *Justice* is what Christian love does when it is confronted by more than one neighbour. Justice, in other words, is an instrument of neighbour love. Justice carries out in the social realm the motivations of love for neighbour.

We can understand what is meant by 'love your neighbour' when we can think of our neighbours one by one in terms of single relationships. But what can 'love your neighbour' mean in national terms? It means that we must seek to express our love for all our neighbours by facilitating justice. Likewise, love for enemies in national and social terms can be expressed in the quest for justice in our dealings with them, and for the vindication of justice in our conflicts with them. Part of the expression of neighbour love, even for enemies, in social and political terms is the quest for, and sometimes enforcement of, justice. As Richard Harries put it: 'Part of the way we show love for our enemy is by not letting injustice succeed.'[10]

What, then, is peace?

'Peace' has become a word of many meanings. In the 'peace movements' it has come to be synonymous with unilateral renunciation of nuclear weapons. In many minds, peace is defined negatively as the absence of hostilities. We hear reference to the Pax Atomica — the unsteady peace of co-existence maintained by a mutual balance of terror. What does 'peace' mean?

Once again, our first task is to define peace *theologically*. Only then can we understand the sort of peace for which Christians are called to be 'peacemakers'.

The Lord *is* Peace! So Gideon's altar to the Lord was built to testify (Jdg.6:24). The Lord *brings* peace, as the prophet's vision of the Coming King makes vividly clear: 'For every boot of the tramping warrior in battle tumult and every garment rolled in blood will be burned as fuel for the fire. For to us a child is born . . . and his name will be called . . . "Prince of Peace". Of the increase of his government and of peace there will be no end' (Is.9:5ff.). But what is 'peace'?

The peace of Messiah's kingdom is not simply the ending of hostilities, not simply the burning of the warrior's boot. The kingdom of peace is established and upheld 'with justice and with righteousness' (Is.9:7). The Old Testament word for peace, *shalom*, covers much more than merely the absence of war. *Shalom* is rather the absence of disorder at all levels of life and relationship. *Shalom* includes everything God gives for human well-being in all areas of life. It means well-being in the widest sense of the word. When the Lord brings peace there is prosperity (Ps.72:1–7), there is health (Is.57:19), there is conciliation (Gn.26:29), there is contentedness (Gn.15:15; Ps.4:8). When the peace of the Lord is present, there are good relationships between nations and men (1 Ch.12:17–18). God's *shalom* peace has both a personal and a social aspect. 'Seek the welfare (*shalom*) of the city where I have sent you into exile,' writes Jeremiah, 'and pray to the LORD on its behalf, for in its welfare you will find your welfare' (Je.29:7).

Peace, then, is about being in right relationships, but it is more even than that. 'Peace' at its highest is about the *enjoyment* and *satisfaction* of being in right relationships – with God, with neighbour, with oneself, with one's environment. True peace is inseparably linked to righteousness: there is no peace without justice, but peace goes beyond justice. Frequently 'peace' and 'righteousness' are bracketed together (Ps.85:10; Is.48:18). And after the exile and the failure of the false prophets to bring a true word of peace (Ezk.13:10,16), the prophetic vision grows of the time when God's anointed will bring in a new kingdom of righteous peace (Is.61:1ff.).

It is of particular interest to see how the Messianic figure in the various sections of Isaiah is depicted as the bringer of peace. The figure introduced as the coming king in Isaiah 9 is described as ruling in peace. In the servant passages in the second part of Isaiah, the suffering servant brings peace to the people (53:5; 55:12) through his costly self-giving. In the final sections, the Messianic figure now dons the garments of the conqueror who establishes peace by fighting for justice (*cf.* Is.59:8ff.).

God's peace, then, will *ultimately* mean the absence of war, but such peace is not promised in the present world order. In fact, we even find 'peace' in the victory of war. Gideon spoke to the men of Penuel of his coming 'in peace . . .', meaning after his *victory* (Jdg.8:9; *cf.* 1 Ki.22:27). Peace can sometimes signify 'victory' – a peace which can only be established through conflict. Peace is about human welfare and human wholeness. Peace is the absence of injustice and 'the fruit of righteousness': as the prophet wrote: 'The effect of right- eousness will be peace' (Is.32:17).

It is this conception of the Lord's *shalom* which underlies the New Testament references to peace. The birth of John the Baptist (Lk.1:79) and then of Jesus himself (Lk.2:14) signal the dawn of an age in which the peace of God can be established. The Messiah's age, which culminates in the end of all wars and in the establishment of a kingdom of right- eousness, begins with the birth of Christ. The evidence for the presence of his kingdom among the disciples is described in terms of the Messianic gift of *shalom* (Lk.7:18ff.). The disciples of the kingdom are to be peacemakers (Mt.5:9). In their personal relationships and within their fellowship, Christians are to be at peace (Mk.9:50).

The peace of the Messiah is thus becoming a reality in the ministry of Jesus. In his healing miracles, Jesus brings peace (Mk.5:34; Lk.7:50). His gospel of peace was the message of the early church (Acts 10:36). But these healings and good deeds pointed beyond merely physical or psychological maturing; they pointed towards the basis of all true peace, *the restoration of a relationship of peace between man and God*. It is to that fundamental restoration of relationship with God, to the removal of disorder from within the human heart, that the prophets of old referred in their vision of the day when swords would be beaten into ploughshares, and spears into pruning hooks. It is that restoration which is made available in Christ (Rom.5; Eph.2:14–17). The 'peace of God' which passes all human understanding and garrisons heart and mind is peace 'in Christ Jesus' (Phil.4:7). It is his gift of peace which he leaves with us, but not as the world gives (Jn.14:27). Such peace is related to his 'overcoming' of the world through the costly conflict of the cross. It is as he shows his disciples his wounded hands and side that he says 'Peace' (Jn.20:19–23, 26; *cf.* Jn.16:33).

God, then, is a 'God of peace' (Phil.4:9). His disciples are to be peacemakers. But the peace of God is founded upon justice and righteousness – ultimately, the justice and righteousness of a right relationship with God in Christ. This is a much deeper peace than the 'peace' of the 'Peace Movements'; it is very far also from the 'Pax Atomica' which is an unsteady peace of non-hostility and co-existence. The peace between man and God which 'passes all understanding' can and should lead to a ministry of reconciliation between others and God, and to a ministry of reconciliation between separated groups (such as Jews and Gentiles for whom Christ is Peace: Eph.2:14). The wholeness of life to which *shalom* refers, however, comes through, and sometimes only through, the establishment of the kingdom of God. Peace involves the establishment of the justice of the kingdom in the face of evil.

The Christian is called to be a peacemaker (Mt.5:9). In its fullest sense, this means working for the peace which is found in God through Christ. It is a calling to share the gospel of peace. But as part of that task, and a part of the work of justice to which he is also called, and with which such peace is linked, the Christian must also work for the more limited peace of co-existence, of conciliation, of restraint in the conflicts of human power. This is not the deep peace of Christ. It is an anxious peace, a fearful peace, a fragile peace.

But it is an essential part of the protecting and ordering of society within the requirements of justice to which a Christian is committed under God. To be a peacemaker, then, will include working for the social structures which make for peace (*shalom*), structures which embody justice. As Wolterstorff puts it, 'We owe it to God and to our fellow human beings to see to it that our society's array of institutions adequately serves the life of its members – that they serve the cause of justice and shalom.'[11]

As we said earlier, one of the provisions of God for the maintenance of order and for the establishment of justice in the fallen world is the institution of the state. We now see that it is to be an institution with certain goals and limits defined by our Christian understanding of order and justice and peace. It is to a fuller theology of the state that we now turn.

Notes for chapter nine

[1] E. W. Heaton, *The Hebrew Kingdoms* (OUP, 1968), p.184.
[2] J. Calvin, *Institutes*, II.ii.5.
[3] L. B. Smedes, *Mere Morality* (Eerdmans, 1983).
[4] N. Wolterstorff, *Until Justice and Peace Embrace* (Eerdmans, 1983), p.81.
[5] P. Ramsey, *Basic Christian Ethics* (Scribners & SCM, 1950), chapter 1.
[6] K. Barth, *Church Dogmatics*, **2** (1) (T. & T. Clark, English Translation, 1955), p.386.
[7] *Third Way*, **6** (10), November 1983.
[8] H. Thielicke, *Theological Ethics*, **2** (English Translation, Eerdmans, 1969), p.616.
[9] P. Ramsey, *op.cit.*, p.92f.
[10] R. Harries (ed.), *What Hope in an Armed World?* (Pickering and Inglis, 1982), p.107.
[11] N. Wolterstorff, *op.cit.*, p.62.

10 Church and state under God

It is now time to look in more detail at that particular provision of God in the fallen world for the maintenance of order and justice, namely the state.

If, at the personal level, we answer the question 'Why are there wars?' by saying that human nature is warlike, at the social and national level the answer has to be given in terms of the nature of states, the problem of state sovereignty and the sorts of values states believe are worth fighting for.

In this section we will try to develop a theology of the state. We will indicate first how differing approaches between Christians to the questions of war are to a large degree dependent on their different attitudes to the relationship of a Christian to the state. Then we will look in some detail at the New Testament teaching on the state, concentrating on the attitude of Jesus to the Jewish state of his day, and those of Paul and of the author of Revelation to the Roman states of their days. We will summarize certain theological principles and look at their relevance to our different world of modern sovereign states. Then, in Chapter 11, we shall ask what light the New Testament throws on the relationship of a Christian citizen to his state.

Christian disagreements

One of the major areas of disagreement between Christians of the 'just war' tradition and many Christian pacifists (often from the Anabaptist traditions) concerns the relationship of the Christian church and the Christian citizen to the secular state authority. Whereas in medieval Christendom there was a virtual popular identification of the Christian church with the state, the major reformers were forced to reconsider in a radical way the roles of church and state under God.

Luther's doctrine of the 'Two Kingdoms' was one way of coping with the 'tension' of living for God in this fallen world. The church and the state (he taught) are both realms in which the active God is at work. In the realm of the church (the kingdom 'on God's right hand'), God is at work through the gospel. The state is God's kingdom 'on the left hand', with authority and power as the minister of God to restrain evil and to maintain justice and order. Luther insisted that these two kingdoms must not be confused.

Calvin shared Luther's belief that God had established two governments for man, the spiritual and the temporal, God ruling in the church through the Word, and through the state by the power of the magistrate's sword. In the *Institutes* Calvin writes:

> Civil government has its appointed end, so long as we live among men, to cherish and protect the outward worship of God, to defend sound doctrine of piety and the position of the church, to adjust our life to the society of men, to form our social behaviour to civil righteousness, to reconcile us with one another, and to promote general peace and tranquillity.[1]

All of this, he agrees, would be superfluous if God's kingdom were to wipe out this present life; but while we are pilgrims here on earth, we need civil government for the sake of our very humanity. Calvin goes further than Luther in requiring that the state 'defend doctrine'; he shares Luther's view that the state was established on account of sin, to restrain evil, to be an organ of providence in ordering our material life, and an instrument of justice for the preservation of the human race in peace and tranquillity. The Church of England clearly owes much to the influence of the continental reformers in the wording of its Article 27, affirming the royal supremacy in matters ecclesiastical or civil, understood in terms of the 'prerogative which we see to have been given always to all godly princes in Holy Scriptures by God himself'. Both church and state are 'under God'.

It is easy to see how in the reformers' views the sanctioning of force, indeed the necessity for the coercive use of force by the civil authority, derives from the understanding of the state as the realm of God's rule ('on the left hand') by the sword. The spiritual concerns of the church are the gospel, and its power is the Word. The temporal concerns of the state are social justice, and its power is the sword.

These main-line reformers had their opponents. The radicals, often called 'Anabaptists', insisted on a re-evaluation of the very concepts of both church and state. There were fringe cranks, as with many movements, but there were many spiritually mature leaders as well. They desired the emergence of a true spiritual community separate from the 'world', which would render ecclesiastical forms unnecessary, and the state as an instrument of power superfluous. This was their prayer. They were committed to practical personal holiness of life and believed the state and its powers to be evil.[2] So oaths and civil office were not for the saints. The Christian community could have no part in these so-called 'agencies of the devil'. Necessarily, therefore, by regarding any state function as inappropriate or wrong for the Christian community, they were also committed to a refusal of military service.

One of the crucial areas of disagreement between these two approaches is seen in the question of the interpretation of the Sermon on the Mount, especially Matthew chapter 5. For the Reformed traditions, the Sermon is understood in continuity with the moral teaching of the Old Testament, describing a pattern of Christian love and godly character, and giving our Lord's radical interpretation of the inner meaning of Old Testament law in contradistinction to various scribal interpretations which stayed with the letter of the law and not its inner heart. Here we are given a description of the character of Christ which both stands over against us, showing up our sin, and is held out before us as our goal in personal character and interpersonal relations.

For the Anabaptist tradition, the Sermon on the Mount is understood in radical discontinuity with much of the moral teaching of the Old Testament. Jesus is giving us a higher moral law; Jesus is rejecting much of the civil code of Moses' law because it does not measure up to the standards of his kingdom. Here we have a new law of life for believers in every sphere of life: personal, social, business, political. The politics of Jesus are radically different from the politics of this world. His teaching requires the renunciation of force, and the refusal to resist one who is evil; this is to be taken with absolute literalism in civil as well as in personal life.

It is here, at the interpretation of parts of the New Testament, and because of the different understandings of the nature of the church in relation to the state, that many Christians today are in radical disagreement. Is the church an 'alternative society' which must display righteousness in its own internal dealings, but which must 'come apart' from the rest of society (the 'sect' mentality)? Or is the church the whole people of God seeking to bring the whole of their society under the rule of God and the revelation of his will, within which different spheres and vocations have different functions (the 'church' mentality)? What does being 'in the world but not of the world' mean for Christians today?

How each individual Christian answers these questions will have considerable bearing on how he perceives the Christian response he is called on to make concerning the question of war and preparations for war.

The state in the New Testament

In our own study, we once again start a long way back. We will turn back to the pages of the New Testament and try to understand how its writers perceived the 'state' of their day, and then try to bring those insights to bear on our very different social context.

Much Christian writing on 'church and state' concentrates on Romans 13, in which it seems the 'church' and the 'state' are clearly defined entities. Christians, it would seem from a quick reading, are merely to accept the authority of the state except where it demands the worship which is due to God alone. This sort of approach sometimes tends to lead to a pietistic, non-political sort of Christianity which leans towards an endorsement of the status quo, and towards a generally conservative approach to political issues. Though we will look carefully at Romans 13, we must think more widely as well.

The state in the Gospels
In the Gospels, the state is the Jewish state. It was part of the

Roman empire, but there was considerable discretion given to Jewish local government in the hands of the Sanhedrin. The question of Jesus' relationship to his state is instructive. In the Gospels we are in a very different world from that of Paul and imperial Rome. Jesus was teaching Jews for whom the distinction between 'people of God' and 'state' was very indistinct. They were a 'holy nation'; religion and politics belonged together.

The way Jesus interpreted the authority of the state is also very significant. When challenged about the laws concerning sabbath observance, for example, he replied, '"The sabbath was made for man, not man for the sabbath"' (Mk.2:27). In other words, he interpreted the law in the light of the faith that laws were intended to serve people – to help them be the sort of people God intended. The letter of the law – the authority of the state administration – was there to serve a higher purpose than its own existence. Politics was for people.

Indeed, Jesus' teaching and demeanour were such that his mission was misinterpreted as being a mission of political national liberation. Was he even taken for a zealot? 'We had hoped that he was the one to redeem Israel' (Lk.24:21).

It is not that Jesus ever urged overthrow of the authority of the state: not at all. But he felt able to stand apart from it sufficiently to criticize the exercise of the state when its laws were interpreted in a way that was out of line with God's purposes for human living.

'Render to Caesar'
But did not Jesus acknowledge the authority of the state in that famous discussion with the Pharisees, when they and the Herodians tried to entrap him by asking: Is it lawful to pay taxes to Caesar or not? Should we pay them or should we not? Jesus, however, knowing their hypocrisy, said, '"Why put me to the test? Bring me a coin, and let me look at it. . . . Whose likeness and inscription is this?" They said to him, "Caesar's." Jesus said to them, "Render to Caesar the things

that are Caesar's, and to God the things that are God's." And they were amazed at him' (Mk.12:13ff.).

This paragraph has certainly been interpreted in terms of a distinction between church and state, but it is not clear that this is the best way of understanding it. It could be that Jesus was exposing the hypocrisy of the Pharisees' question by asking for a coin. They had Roman tribute money on them. They were accepting the benefits of Roman rule. So – says Jesus – of course they must pay for these benefits! They can pay tribute to Caesar without being disloyal to God.

Alternatively, the saying could be taken the way Peter Hinchliff takes it in *Holiness and Politics* – an interpretation which goes back to Tertullian. The coin is Caesar's because it bears Caesar's image. But we are to give to God what belongs to God. There is, therefore, an implied series of parallel questions and answers: 'What do we give to God?' 'Why, that which bears his image.' 'And what does bear God's image?' 'Man, of course, as the book of Genesis tells us.' 'The implication is therefore that there is no separation of spheres. The whole of a man bears God's image. The whole of himself is owing to God, including his political life. What he owes to Caesar is a small part of what he is worth. God claims the whole and, therefore, God reigns supreme even over the political sphere.'[3]

Either way, we should not base too much of a theology of the state on this incident. Jesus, as often in his dealings with people, is primarily concerned to tackle the underlying assumptions of his questioners, exposing their hypocrisy. It is not his purpose here to give any straightforward teaching on the state; indeed, he does not really make clear how to distinguish what belongs to Caesar from what belongs to God. It is primarily from the standpoint of our wider theological perspective (particularly from the discussions of the state in Romans 13, to which we shall shortly turn) that we can see that there is nothing which belongs to Caesar which does not also belong to God.

Jesus and Pilate

The encounter between church and state personified in the meeting between Jesus and Pilate is also instructive. Jesus confirms Pilate's claim to have authority: 'You would have no power over me unless it had been given you from above' (Jn.19:11). Even Pilate, acting within a state which was opposed to the truth of Christ, had 'power to release ... power to crucify'. And Jesus says that this power is from God. But Pilate's power is misused in a complete dereliction of duty. Pilate acts not in accordance with the demands of justice (a failure pinpointed in the Gospels by Pilate's wife, Mt.27:19), but in order to 'satisfy the crowd' (Mk.15:15). The evangelists present their accounts with the clear message that Pilate was failing to fulfil his God-given responsibility to ensure justice. Even in that terrible failure, however, the door is opened for the birth of the church through the cross of Christ. Through the institution of the state – albeit even in its failure – God is still at work for good.[4]

The picture emerges of the state having *a derived role*, an authority 'given' by God. The state is there by divine permission, and with a divine commission. But there is no uncritical acceptance and blind submission. Jesus himself faces Pilate with the issue of truth: 'You say that I am a king. For this I was born, and for this I have come into the world, to bear witness to the truth' (Jn.18:37). One of the responsibilities of the church to the state is to bear witness to the truth of Christ. One of the responsibilities of the state, under God, is to maintain justice.

In summary so far, what can we draw from the Gospels about the relation of church and state?

It seems clear that Jesus saw the political sphere as part of the totality of life lived before God. He did not give uncritical acceptance to the state's authority, but recognized its provisional character as an instrument of God's purpose for human life when its laws were directed towards the service of human welfare.

If we now turn back to Romans 13, we find Paul offering a very similar picture.

Paul and Romans 13

There is a recognition, first, that all authority comes from God. Just as the Most High in the prophecy of Daniel is the divine figure who controls world destiny, and gives authority to whom he wills (Dn.7:27), so Paul acknowledges that all human authority is *derived*. 'There is no authority except from God, and those that exist have been instituted by God' (verse 1). The emphasis here is not that all and every exercise of human authority necessarily carries the divine *imprimatur*, but that all human authority is answerable to God and is possibly only because of the authority of God. This is a warning to those in authority, not a carte blanche! It is a warning also to those who would disregard the authorities. Whether we like it or not, those exercising a governing authority in ordering human society have a God-given task.

Secondly, civil government is instituted for the provision of a framework for order and justice, and for the enhancement of human well-being according to God's purpose. This is the positive force of verse 4: 'for he is God's servant, appointed to promote what is good'.[5] As Barrett comments on the word 'servant', behind the more technical use of the term as 'service to the needy' there lies the idea of ministry as seen in the ministry of Jesus himself, and then by him through the church. The state and its officers have a part, therefore, to play in this ministry of Christ.

In negative terms, the state functions as God's servant and instrument of vengeance to carry out his wrath against the man who practises evil. God's wrath is his hostility to and judgment on 'all ungodliness and wickedness of men' (Rom.1:18), which will be revealed in the last day (Rom.2:5) but which can be anticipated in the present. One means for this present expression of his wrath is the sword of the magistrate – which means his authority to inflict the sentence of death.

We must pause briefly on the word used for 'sword' (*machaira*, verse 4). It is often suggested that this refers only to the magistrate's sword of office, and is the word for the small dagger rather than the sword used in war. Some Christians argue from this that Paul could not therefore have had any thought of warfare in mind in his reference to the sword, but only of police activity within the state itself. Whether or not warfare was in Paul's mind here, we need to be clear that 'sword' is the word used for violent death in Romans 8:35 and Hebrews 11:37 (*cf.* also Acts 12:2; 16:27; Rev.13:10), and although its primary reference may be to the magistrate's symbol of office, it must also include his right to use the sword in the infliction of death if necessary. (This is not to argue for the propriety or wisdom of capital punishment in our society, nor to suggest that the magistrate's use of the sword is necessarily the death penalty exclusively. However, it is to say that in Paul's argument, the deterrent effect of the 'sword' carried by the magistrate depends on his right to use it in some circumstances.)

So the state in Paul's thinking in Romans 13 is an aspect of God's providential ordering of the world within which his wrath is given expression as his resistance to evil. The state itself is given authority to bring the wrath of God to bear upon evil doers. As Barrett again notes[6], paradoxically this is also an instrument of God's longsuffering (Rom.2:4), for through this particular manifestation of God's wrath through the magistrate, the power of evil is restrained and its final judgment deferred.

Romans 13 was written in the early years of the reign of Nero; it is not clear that Paul would necessarily have given wholly the same emphasis a few years later. It is important, also, to notice how this chapter immediately follows Romans 12. We will come back to this shortly, to explore the distinction between what is proper to the private citizen and what is proper to the state. But here we notice that it is precisely through proper respect for, and obedience to, the state's authority that expression is given in terms of public responsibility to the duties of Christian neighbour love, and rejection of retaliation (Rom.12:9f.). This is not, however, to say that blind obedience is required by the Christian to every particular government which happens to be in power. It is rather that the principle of ordered government for the protection of justice, the furtherance of good and the resistance of evil is ordained by God.

Revelation 13

When imperial Rome later, under Domitian, became oppressively totalitarian, and the emperor demanded the worship of his citizens, the biblical author described that state then in terms of a demonic monster. In Revelation 13 we are given a theological interpretation of a tyrannical regime. The monster was 'granted power' from above (verse 7), even though it 'rose from the sea', having its origin in the demonic depths. Here is a bestial revolt against order, a tyrannical regime demanding the worship of its citizens. This is a state that has exceeded its God-given functions, and failed to exercise its God-given responsibilities. It has thus become demonic.

Revelation 13 describes a system of ideological tyranny. Thielicke describes it in terms of the 'self-absolutization of a creaturely phenomenon and the resultant ideology'.[7] Here is the reduction of the human spirit to a mere instrument for the practical exercise of power. Here is the establishment of the state as a secular anti-church. In such a system, the state goes beyond its lawful bounds and claims the whole man. Its ideology has as its goal the advancement of its own power. Chapter 13 of Revelation serves as a warning that totalitarian regimes, by exceeding their rightful functions, become demonic, and that the power of the state can be used for evil instead of for good. Even then, however, like Cyrus the Persian pagan anointed to act in God's name in the political arena (Is.45:1), the state itself remains under the sovereign authority of the Lord, to whom the nations are 'like a drop from a bucket' (Is.40:15).

Notes for chapter ten

[1] J. Calvin, *Institutes*, IV.xx.2.
[2] Although the New Testament itself gives evidence of the existence of state institutions, such as courts, in *e.g.* 1 Cor.5 and 6; 2 Cor.13.
[3] Peter Hinchliff, *Holiness and Politics* (DLT, 1982), p.4.
[4] *Cf.* J. Atkinson, *Church and State under God* (Latimer Studies, 1983).
[5] C. K. Barrett, *The Epistle to the Romans* (A. & C. Black, 1957), p.246.
[6] *Ibid.*
[7] H. Thielicke, *Theological Ethics*, **2** (English Translation, Eerdmans, 1969), p.54.

11 Christian citizens today

It is, of course, not easy to draw direct lines from the Jewish state which Jesus knew, or the authoritarian imperial Rome of Paul's day, to our Western democracies. In many ways the modern 'sovereign state', with its implicit or explicit claims to a total ordering of all means of life, has parallels with the 'religious function' of the states in the New Testament. But modern democratic states are not religious institutions in the same way as states were in the ancient world. Indeed, the secular world view of the modern state, although making some claim to allegiance from its members, is limited to this world, and has no awareness of the next.

It is perhaps easier to see direct lines between the totalitarian system of Domitian's Rome described in Revelation, and modern totalitarian ideological systems. In such, we may discern implicit claims of the state to be a 'pseudo-church', with a total demand on the minds and souls of its citizens, and with a concentration of power directed primarily towards its own self-perpetuation. But what of democracies? Democratic government is not 'given' in the way authority was given to Caesar in Rome. As electors, we all have a measure of responsibility for it. It is not simply a matter of whether or not to 'obey'. We now have a constitutionally provided 'opposition to government'. The question of resistance to the state's authority is now couched in different terms. And with the underlying social changes in industrial monopolies, power vested in trades unions and in the media, universal education with its own hidden curricula and presuppositions, and so on, the locus of power in our democracy is a far more complicated question than in the ancient world.

Nevertheless, while we cannot draw direct lines from the patterns of government in the New Testament to those of today, the officers of state and elected representatives do bear responsibility for governing. It is at this point that the New Testament principles defining the purposes for which governments exist in the purposes of God do have relevance for the institutions of our very different Western democracies.

Let us try to summarize:

The authority vested in government is part of the purposes of God for maintaining order within a disordered and fallen world. The state is therefore subordinate to God and his laws.

The state is never an ultimate authority, but is responsible before God for the exercise of its authority.

The state has a provisional and limited role within this present age.

The state is God's minister; it exists for the people, not for its own sake as a dominating force.

The need governments meet is the need of justice, and hence the need to ensure a context of order in which justice can be established.

The order and law for which the state is responsible is rooted in morality, and hence in the character of the Creator: it is not an arbitrary creation of government. The rule of government has to be seen in the light of a more ultimate order.

When separated, as in totalitarian regimes, from the authority given by God, and especially when it oversteps its real – God-imposed – limits by trying to act as a 'church' as well, the state becomes demonic, and its power can be wrongly used for evil instead of good.

Our world is now constituted by those tightly-defined entities which are our modern states, which tend to be characterized by the insistence of each nation to have a state of its own. Despite the theoretical attractiveness of such a principle, however, as Wolterstorff points out, it inevitably leads in our modern world to injustice and conflict.

> The crux of what goes wrong is that states are of course territorial entities, and nowhere in the modern world are the inhabitants of the territory belonging to a state the members of just one nation. Consequently, when one nation has a state of its own, there will nevertheless always be citizens of that state who are not members of the nation, and these people will be left with only two choices: either to emigrate, under varying degrees of duress, or to accept the status of second-class citizens, with varying degrees of deprivation of rights and of repression. *There is never any other choice.*[1]

The problems in South Africa and with the Palestinians are cited as clear examples.

One of the God-given tasks of government, therefore, must be to seek to establish structures which maximize the possibilities for justice and for *shalom* within societies and between societies.

The state, then, can be one instrument in God's hands for the curbing of man's aggressiveness which threatens to destroy his creativity, and for the promotion of justice and order within which human life can flourish. Justice needs a framework of order. It is from this basis that Paul's reference to the 'sword' must be understood as the propriety of using coercive force, in certain circumstances, for the maintenance of order and for the sake of justice. As Richard Harries put it:

> Life is characterised by the clash of self-interest and sometimes by brutality, rapacity, and malevolence. Such

characteristics make coercive government necessary. Human beings are also moved by love, loyalty and altruism, and we would come together naturally to organise our corporate existence, because we are social beings. But the state as we know it, the state with coercive power, is at once the result of and a remedy for our limited capacity to take other people into account. Because we are liable to realise our own interests at the expense of other people, coercive government is essential. It sets limits to the harm we can do.[2]

State and citizen

Does all this mean that it is sometimes right for the state to do what it would be wrong for an individual Christian to do? We must now discuss this briefly, and begin with the simple point that Romans 13 comes just after Romans 12!

In Romans chapter 12, Paul begins to draw out the ethical implications of the gospel of grace he has been expounding for the first eleven chapters. The argument is concluded: by receiving the gift of God's love, and being united to Christ by faith in the crucified and risen Jesus, a person, whether Jew or Gentile, can be set free from the paralysing powers of sin and guilt and fear and death to be their true self in obedience to God's will. On the basis of the grace of God which enables this liberating gospel, Paul appeals to his Christian readers in Rome, those now part of the new family born of God's love and confessing Christ as Lord, that they live differently. 'Don't let the world around you squeeze you into its own mould' (Rom.12:1ff., J. B. Phillips).

Paul then goes on to express what the newness of life will mean in certain contexts. In the Christian community which is the Body of Christ, the believer is to have a right assessment of himself and his gifts, and use what God has given for the common good (verses 3–8). His life is to be marked by the sort of love which is hospitable and seeks the good of the other. Then, surely in conscious dependence on the teaching of Christ which the Gospels have preserved in the Sermon on the Mount, Paul goes on: 'Bless those who persecute you; bless and do not curse them' (verse 14; *cf*. Lk.6:28). Live in harmony with others and in humility. 'Repay no one evil for evil' (verse 17; *cf*. here Mt.5:38–42; Lk.6:29). 'Beloved, never avenge yourselves, but leave it to the wrath of God' (verse 19); rather, 'if your enemy is hungry, feed him; if he is thirsty, give him drink; for by so doing you will heap burning coals on his head.' This follows Barrett's interpretation of the verse, in view of Paul's reference to overcoming evil with good in verse 21. 'Do not be overcome by evil, but overcome evil with good' (verses 20–21).

In other words, in personal relations the Christian is to have no place for revenge or retaliation. 'The wrath' is God's judgment on evil. And the exercise of 'the wrath' is God's prerogative alone. 'No private person is at liberty to assume that his own vengeful feelings will carry out the divine sentence.'[3] Vengeance is reserved to God.

When we turn over to chapter 13, we find references again to good and evil (verses 3,4) and again to the exercise of the wrath of God on the evildoer (verse 4). But here the state is divinely appointed as God's servant, the human agency through which the divine sentence can be carried out. The state may do what a private individual in personal relationships may not do, namely express the judgment of God upon evil.

The tendency among some pacifist writers (especially of the Anabaptist tradition) to insist that the Sermon on the Mount is meant to be interpreted to cover both personal and civil relationships will not therefore hold. Here Paul is moving from a dependence on the Sermon on the Mount in his teaching about personal relationships, to a discussion of the Christian citizen's responsibility to those in authority in the Roman state, and he is allowing even the anti-Christian Roman state's exercise of the sword to be understood as a divinely ordained instrument in God's service.

Nor will it do, therefore, to suggest that although the state may have a God-given duty in some circumstances to use the sword, Christians can have no part in that work. Such a view, common among pacifist writers, seeks to acknowledge the importance of civil government on the one hand, while denying Christian involvement on the other.

It seems much clearer to make a distinction, not between the Christian and the state, but between the Christian's responsibilities as a private individual in personal relationships, and his official responsibilities as a citizen of the state. In both, no personal vengeance nor retaliation is permitted to him, but whereas in the former, his duty is not to 'repay evil with evil', not to 'avenge himself', but to 'leave it to the wrath of God' (Rom.12:17ff.), in the latter he may be called to assume office as the servant of God (Rom.13:4), to exercise judgment against evildoers who threaten order and justice. To recall our discussion of the Sermon on the Mount, Jesus was not rejecting Christian involvement in the proper administration of justice. He was, however, forbidding the individual to take the law into his own hands.[4]

From our discussion so far, it is clear that the extent to which an individual Christian may decide to share in the God-given tasks entrusted to the state is a matter for his individual conscience and vocation. Against the Christian traditions which urge 'come apart and be separate', our reading of the New Testament endorses the view expressed by *Gaudium et Spes* at the Second Vatican Council:

> It is fully consonant with human nature that there should be politico-juridical structures providing all citizens without any distinction with ever-improving and effective opportunities to play an active part in the establishment of the juridical foundations of the political community, in the administration of public affairs, in determining the aims and terms of reference of public bodies, and in the election of political leaders ... The Church praises and esteems those who devote themselves to the public good for the service of men and take upon themselves the burdens of public office.[5]

To say, however, that the state may do what a private individual may not do, namely express God's wrath in justice to the individuals who do evil, is not to say that the state is not under a rule of morality. On the contrary, the state's law has to be understood in the light of the moral character of God, from which personal morality also is derived. It is not that the individual is under moral constraint, and the state is not. Both are answerable to God, but both have different responsibilities in the appropriate expression of his character.

It is part of the church's responsibility to the state to make clear God's revelation of his character and his truth, and to hold leaders of government accountable to him in their heavy responsibility for decision-making.

Notes for chapter eleven

[1] N. Wolterstorff, *Until Justice and Peace Embrace* (Eerdmans, 1983), p.114.
[2] R. Harries (ed.), *What Hope in an Armed World?* (Pickering & Inglis, 1982), p.88.
[3] C. K. Barrett, *The Epistle to the Romans* (A. & C. Black, 1957), p.242.
[4] *Cf*. J. R. W. Stott, *Christian Counter-Culture* (IVP, 1978), p.113.
[5] Second Vatican Council, *Gaudium et Spes* (December 1965), section 75 in A. Flannery (ed.), *The Conciliar and Post-Conciliar Documents* (Fowler Wright Books, Ltd, 1981).

12 Force, power and forgiveness

At the end of Chapter 4 we isolated three particular spectra of views on which Christians have come to different conclusions. The first concerned the nature of man, and whether or not he was basically trustworthy. We have argued that fallen man, though still bearing God's image, is to a large degree given up to mistrust and aggressiveness, and that restraints are therefore needed in the exercise of his powers. The second concerned the relationship between church and state. We have argued that the state has an important, positive, yet limited God-given role in maintaining a context of order and justice in the fallen world for the sake of the continuance of human life, and for the possibility of movement towards a righteous peace. It is time now to look at the third spectrum of views on which Christians have come to different conclusions, namely: Where is the cut-off point in the state's use of force?

Coercive force

The social order which justice requires and from which peace can grow will sometimes only be maintained by the coercive use of force against those who fragment it. Coercive government is a result of and to some extent a remedy for man's basic tendency to self-interest. That this is accepted by Paul is shown in the understanding of the Roman state which emerges in the discussion of Romans 13. The authority is 'God's servant for your good . . . an instrument of vengeance to carry out God's wrath against the man who practises evil'.[1] In that context, it is 'not for nothing that he bears a sword' – the reference to the authority of the magistrate even in inflicting the sentence of death. The picture is of the policing role of government for the sake of order and justice, and Paul's concern is that Christian believers in Rome should acknowledge the provision of such government as divinely ordained.

At this point we recall from our earlier discussion of power that God's exercise of his divine power is to be understood as an expression of his holy love. Likewise – to give another example – the use of coercive force in family discipline may and must sometimes be exercised for the sake of love. So also in the state, operating within its God-given limits, we will argue that some exercise of power (for example in punishing criminals) for the sake of maintaining order and justice can be seen as an expression of God's loving provision for the fallen world.

But are there any limits to the state's exercising of its power? In particular, may the acceptance of the use of force in the restraint of the criminal within society be extrapolated to the use of force against aggression from without? Can the state use the 'sword' of war against external enemies?

In Chapter 3 we quoted Calvin's justification of some wars based on his extrapolation from the magistrate's use of the sword in Romans 13. 'Princes must be armed not only to restrain the misdeeds of private individuals by judicial punishment, but also to defend by war the dominions entrusted to their safe-keeping if at any time they are under enemy attack.'[2] The grounds for his extrapolation are both 'natural equity' and 'the nature of the political office'. To such an argument might be added the consideration, expressed by the psalmist's praise to God, that 'vindication [of justice] in the sight of the nations' (Ps.98:1,2) through victory against God's enemies, is part of God's 'marvellous work'.

However, as we have seen, what Calvin means by 'war' is very far from the violence and indiscriminate destruction of modern technological warfare. It is even less easy to find grounds for praise in the style of the psalmist under today's shadow of the mushroom cloud. It is still open to us to ask to what extent extrapolation to questions of modern warfare from Romans 13 is valid.

The issue can be divided into a question of duties and a question of means. It seems clear that if the state has a God-given duty in maintaining order and establishing justice, then if its order is threatened by attack from an external enemy, there is an implied God-given duty to seek to maintain its security. In other words, the state has a duty to defend its citizens against unjust aggression. This seems inescapable from the requirements of the covenant made with Noah: God requires life to be preserved and the conditions for life's preservation to be upheld. This seems a valid deduction also from Paul's argument in Romans 13. Defence is part of the proper function of the state, in which government has responsibility for the safety of its citizens.

However, the question of *means* is a separate one. We need first to recall the fact that God used different means throughout the history of his people for the maintenance of order. In the narrative of Genesis 9, the death penalty is prescribed for murder. Elsewhere in the pentateuchal laws, capital punishment is prescribed for certain crimes. The 'blood revenge' is a solemn duty. However, with the development of the desert community into a tribal confederacy, and eventually into an established monarchy, the practice of punishment changed. As early as Hosea's day in the eighth century BC, the death penalty was apparently not enforced for adultery: the appropriate response seems to have been divorce. Later, in Jesus' day, the incident recorded in John 8 also illustrates the fact that stoning for adultery was not then enforced. We could argue likewise in the case of war. The 'holy war' of Judges and the defensive wars of the monarchy are worlds away from the grudging toleration of Roman rule which marked the time of Jesus.

While we may affirm that the proper concern of the state is the preservation of life in order and justice, which necessarily includes the defence of its people, it does not necessarily follow that war is inevitably a requirement of that defence. In our world there are possibilities of trade and economic sanctions, of diplomatic co-operation and diplomatic pressure, quite unknown to Paul, or even Calvin. There are different sanctions available for restraining and punishing the aggressor than an immediate or inevitable resort to war.

We need to be careful, therefore, in any extrapolation we make from Romans 13, and from too easy an assumption that 'the sword' justifies war. However, there may be occasions when it may be judged that the order and security of the state could be secured, or justice vindicated, *by no other means* than a defensive use of force. Such a course could then be seen as an emergency decision of the state, a last resort thrust on it from outside. It would involve an acceptance of the need for the use of force as an evil measure undertaken to avert a greater evil. In such circumstances may the state then exercise force to the extent of taking life? May the state kill? What is a Christian assessment of such violence?

It is at this point that the spectrum of views emerges, and

the cut-off point in the use of force becomes the issue of disagreement. Some Christian pacifists could follow the argument right up to the point of agreeing that the state may use some degree of force in a defensive way against aggression, but draw the line at killing. Others believe that there are circumstances in which the state is empowered to take the lives of aggressors, arguing that this is morally equivalent to the capital punishment for criminals within society which Romans 13 seems to allow. (Whether or not capital punishment *is* the appropriate response of modern states to certain categories of criminal is not being argued here.)

We will give examples of some different viewpoints.

Christ and violence

There are Christians who have sought, and do seek, justification in the Christian gospel for the use of violence, particularly in the face of tyranny. One of the clearest paragraphs comes from the pen of Jurgen Moltmann, who urges that love sometimes *requires* the use of force:

> It is not the idealistic principle of non-violence that is consonant with the Gospel, but the responsible action of love. Love is divine power-in-weakness (2 Cor.12:9). Responsible political action in love is selfless to the point of sacrifice of personal innocence, to the point of incurring guilt. From this we are led to the following conclusions: first, non-violence in the sense of non-resistance cannot be justified in tyrannical situations, because it permits and encourages violence. It does not save the personal innocence of the individual, but leads to 'more irredeemable guilt'. Second, violence, construed as the love which desires to put an end to evil, cannot be approved but it can be answered for. Resistance may not triumph over its victims. It is revenge not love which does that. Guilt remains guilt, but in faith we can live with this guilt and need not commit suicide. The engagement to resist remains a 'bitter engagement'. But in this instance too the incurring of guilt

in the responsible love which has recourse to counter-violence cannot be restricted to the case of resistance. It is only that the example of resistance reveals the factors which secretly and often unconsciously determine all political action. Third, it follows from this that action and failure to act are not the same in such situations in the sense that either way one incurs guilt. There is the 'more irredeemable guilt' which in most cases consists of sins of omission.[3]

Theology of liberation

The theology of liberation, especially in its South American form, also takes up this theme. Beginning with the situation of oppression, the cries of suffering of those whose misery stems primarily from being at the 'periphery' of the world economic system, the liberation theologians move to an analysis of the structures which perpetuate social misery. People are being wronged. They are being deprived of their sustenance rights, their benefit rights, their freedom rights. They are being oppressed because of economic and political domination of rich countries. Those in the 'periphery' see the 'core' not as benefactors, but as predators. Such theologies would agree with Wolterstorff's comment which we quoted before: 'We do in fact live in a world-system in which the core dominates the periphery, characteristically out of greed and a lust for power. What is that but sin? We do in fact live in a world-system shaped by the practice of treating economic growth as an autonomous and ultimate good. What is that but idolatry?'[4]

The theologies of liberation go on to argue that if sin is manifest in oppressive social structures, and if salvation is ultimately liberation from sin, then the struggle to eliminate unjust structures has significance in the story of salvation. The Christian quest for justice, say these theologies, *requires* the struggle for justice by the 'periphery' against the 'core'.

What form such struggle should take leads to disagreement. Some, in line with the thinking of some of the reformers, argue that active resistance against repression can take the form of civil disobedience: a notoriously unjust ruler can forfeit his claim to office, and no longer has a claim on a citizen's obedience. Others go further and argue for the legitimacy of violent resistance against oppression, for the sake of the vindication of the rights of the poor. There is much more Christian discussion needed on whether or not such violence could be morally permissible.

It seems unmistakably clear, from an examination of the Sermon on the Mount and elsewhere, that in a Christian's personal relationships with his fellow men he is to renounce all exercise of power or retaliation in his own defence. He is to 'turn the other cheek'; he is not to 'resist' one who is evil. Here his model is the powerlessness of Christ, who renounced his own status, limiting the exercise of his power for the sake of others whom he loved (Phil.2:5ff.).

The situation becomes much more complicated, however, when 'evil' is being perpetrated not against oneself alone, but also against others for whom one is responsible. Here to 'resist not one who is evil' may in fact be to acquiesce in injustice against another neighbour. When more than one neighbour is involved, the question of neighbour love becomes: 'How can the law of love be translated into terms of social policy, order and justice?' Is Moltmann right, then, that responsible love sometimes *requires* the use of violence in the resistance of 'one who is evil', particularly if the evil is being practised against one for whom we have a responsibility?

Power and love

This brings us back to what Thielicke calls 'the decisive ethical problem'.[5] We are back to the problem of Christian ethics 'after the flood'. We are back to the 'ethical borderline'. On the one hand, as Christians we are under the command of Christ to love even our enemies. And there are no limits to that command. We cannot make the exercise of power in human institutions a separate sort of activity outside the range of Christ's command. On the other hand, as we have seen, the fallen world – and fallen man within it – needs an ordering restraint, in other words we need institutions empowered to restrain and order.

Power and love cannot, therefore, be mutually exclusive. As Thielicke puts it: 'Love is the fundamental motive on the basis of which and in the name of which power is both exercised and limited; indeed, love is the motive which validates the rule of power in the Noachic covenant.'[6] Quoting Luther, Thielicke continues, 'In the fallen world, which admittedly needs power in order to restrain evil, this restraint of evil is understood wholly in terms of the motive of paternal and sustaining love. For in an uncontrolled play of mere forces it would be the weak and miserable who would get crushed. It is in order to defend *them* against injustice, to extend paternal love to *them* that God provides the protection of force. Thus in equipping the state with punitive power, *e.g.*, God is actually expressing love, for in doing so he takes the weak, oppressed and persecuted under his wing.'[7]

In other words, *there are different ways of expressing love*. In the more personal I-Thou relationships, love is primarily expressed through the surrender of power, and the exercise of gentleness and mercy (although, of course, discipline in family life can also be part of love). In the more public and institutional spheres, the 'manner' of love is primarily evident in what Luther calls its 'alien' work of judging, punishing and repressing evil (although mercy and forgiveness can also be part of institutional life). As Paul Tillich said,

> It is the alien work of love to destroy what is against love.
> . . . Love, in order to exercise its proper works, namely charity and forgiveness, must provide for a place in which this can be done, through its strange work of judging and punishing. In order to destroy what is against love, love must be united with power, and not only with power, but also with compulsory power.[8]

God's work of love is expressed through human loves, again in a variety of manners. 'He does the proper work of love by evoking our love through his love, our mercy through his mercy, our forgiveness through his forgiveness (1 Jn.4:10, 19; Mt.18:23–35). And he does the alien work of love by causing human individuals and institutions forcefully to restrain evil.'[9]

So can states kill?

We have seen that the 'sanctity of human life' means that human life is precious, to be respected and normally to be protected. This respect is enshrined in the command 'Thou shalt do no murder'. We have also seen that there is a severe prohibition against the shedding of innocent blood, and that the Old Testament has clear distinctions in mind between a proper killing of criminals who deserve capital punishment, and the wrongful taking of innocent life. We also understood that the 'sanctity of human life' is not therefore an absolute principle, and that there are occasions when God takes life for the sake of life. Putting these together, we can see that it can be part of the alien work of love in the restraint of evil for appropriate authority to take life in order to preserve life and in order to preserve the conditions under which life may be lived. But 'innocent' life must not be taken; discrimination must be made between what Paul called the 'evildoer' and others. A distinction is to be drawn between just and unjust killing. A distinction must be made, therefore, between just and unjust wars.

It is on such a distinction that the 'just war' theory was developed, and in which its powerful criteria of discrimination and proportion are so crucial. Not only must the '*cause*' of the war be just – which we can now see to be a response of the 'alien work of love' in the face of injustice; a 'just' war may only be a defensive war waged in order to restore order and vindicate justice. The *means* of the waging of war must also be just: *discrimination* has to be made between 'innocent' and 'evildoers'. And 'proportion' has to be observed, such that only the *minimum* force necessary to achieve the goals is used. The just war, therefore, has to be a limited war.

In actual warfare, of course, the edges become blurred, and in modern total warfare the drawing of lines becomes very complicated. We shall look at this further in the next chapter. But the principle of non-combatant immunity is one way of seeking to maintain these criteria. They are ways in which Christian thinkers have tried to give expression to the need for just means in the waging of war.

At this point we should comment briefly on the view, argued by some Christians, that the Old Testament examples of total warfare indicate that God sometimes requires *indiscriminate* elimination of an evil enemy. These people would urge such Old Testament examples as appropriate guidance for today's world.

We argued in Chapter 1 that it is methodologically inadequate to base any binding principle on isolated biblical examples, particularly the specialized Old Testament reference to the 'holy war'. Furthermore, although in his sovereign majesty God could have specifically commanded such an extreme action of retributive justice in the special circumstances of the start of his people's national life, that gives no mandate for Christian action on the same basis, for whom no such specific command is given. Our Christian task is allegiance to the God whose nature is revealed in the Old and New Testaments and supremely in Christ. We are called to neighbour love, and to the justice such love requires. It cannot be right to take to ourselves the prerogative – which belongs if anywhere to God alone – of deciding that a whole people's way of life has become so evil that all alike must suffer equal judgment. For war to be just, it has to be severely limited.

While, therefore, in principle we conclude that in the emergency last resort the state may take the lives of aggressors for the sake of the preservation of the order which makes continuation of life possible, and for the sake of the justice within which God desires life to be lived, we insist that the queston of the justice of the *means* of warfare is all-important. Despite all the difficulties of accurate definition, the criteria of discrimination and proportion remain crucial. Otherwise mass killing may in fact merely be mass murder.

The politics of forgiveness

It would be wrong to interpret Luther's distinction between the 'proper' work of love (seen especially in personal relationships and in family life) and the 'alien' work of love (seen especially in institutional resistance to evil) as a distinction between private and public morality. The same law of love holds for both spheres. It is the *manner* of love which is different. However, just as there is an important place for discipline within the proper love of family life, so there is an important place for mercy within the restraint of evil in political life.

Some recent writers, notably Haddon Willmer[10] and Peter Hinchliff[11], have begun to develop what they call a 'politics of forgiveness'. Their main thesis is that the Christian concept of forgiveness (which as we saw is very closely linked to the biblical conception of justice) indicates certain characteristics of a Christian response to evil which, if they were taken into the political sphere, could give a certain direction to the political agenda. Forgiveness is a dynamic concept of change. It refuses to be trapped into a fatalistic determinism. It acknowledges the reality of evil, wrong and injustice, but it seeks to respond to wrong in a way that is creative of new possibilities. Forgiveness signals an approach to wrong in terms, not of peace at any price, nor of a destructive intention to destroy the wrongdoer, but of a willingness to seek to reshape the future in the light of the wrong, in the most creative way possible. Forgiveness rules out all thought of bare retaliation. Forgiveness underlines the reality of human frailty and sin, and of the limited capacities of human resources to deal with them, but for the sake of the common good it seeks to explore ways of handling present guilt creatively and not destructively. Forgiveness involves a gracious initiative from the one who is wronged. Without forgiveness in the political arena, the options open seem to be *either* to reject the notion that politics is about conciliation and making the best of faulty people, limited resources and a distorting heritage, *or* to abandon all quest for justice and to acquiesce in injustice, accepting any state of affairs. (The most obvious area of application of this principle is in the making of political systems and in the creation of political structures. Willmer's own example is of the political situation in South Africa.)

In our Christian task of trying to formulate the authority and limits of the state under God, and as accountable to him, we need to temper our proper insistence on the right and duty of government to use appropriate coercive force for the sake of order and justice, with the biblical understanding of justice which in Christ so clearly becomes redemptive. Part of the Christian task in politics is to explore how divine justice and forgiveness can transform the expressions of human justice, and so make a state's response to evil both just and redemptive.

Notes for chapter twelve

[1]*Cf.* C. K. Barrett on Romans 13:4 in *The Epistle to the Romans* (A. & C. Black, 1957), p.246.

[2]J. Calvin, *Institutes*, IV.xx.11.

[3]J. Moltmann in C. Brown (ed.), *Dictionary of New Testament Theology*, **3** (Paternoster, 1978), p.971.

[4]Wolterstorff, *Until Justice and Peace Embrace* (Eerdmans, 1983), p.66.

[5]H. Thielicke, *Theological Ethics*, **2** (English Translation, Eerdmans, 1969), p.241.   [6]*Ibid.*, p.242.   [7]*Ibid.*, p.243.

[8]P. Tillich, *Love, Power and Justice* (OUP, 1954), quoted in H. Thielicke, *Theological Ethics*, **2**, p.243.

[9]H. Thielicke, *op.cit.*, p.244.

[10]H. Willmer, 'Politics of Forgiveness' in *Third Way*, **3** (5), May 1979, pp.15–20.

[11]In *Holiness and Politics* (DLT, 1982).

13 'Christus Victor'

We have been discussing the human predicament, and one of God's provisions for the fallen world which is given to maintain a measure of order and justice so that life, and the conditions under which life is to be lived before God, may be preserved. We now conclude by placing this discussion within the wider context of God's purposes for history. What, ultimately, is God doing in his world? How are we to understand our history within the purposes of God? For us, much more sharply than for previous Christian generations, we have to tackle questions like these in their apocalyptic context. What does the Bible tell us about the end of the world itself?

One of the consistent themes of the Old Testament's references to war is the picture of God's opposition to evil and injustice. The New Testament, we saw, also picks up the theme of the warrior God in its discussions of Christ's confrontation with evil, and the calling of the Christian church to a spiritual warfare. The confidence of the Christian in the fight against evil rests in the victory of Christ over all the powers of evil at the cross of Calvary. At the cross, writes Paul, God 'disarmed the principalities and powers and made a public example of them, triumphing over them in him' (Col.2:15). The Christian community is called to enter this victory, although 'the weapons of our warfare are not worldly but have divine power to destroy strongholds' (2 Cor.10:4). The Christian confidence is based in Christ 'who always leads us in triumph' (2 Cor.2:14) – a reference to the 'victory procession' of the conquering hero.

Here, then, we find a double edge to the story of the cross. At the cross of Christ, God's power is manifest against all the forces of evil, triumphing over them, even conquering the power of death itself (1 Cor.15:20). Here is the Christian confidence to don the Christian armour and fight with the weapons of the Spirit against the 'principalities and powers in the heavenly places'. Yet at the cross we also see most markedly the weakness and vulnerability of God. He is defeated, but is not ultimately defeated by defeat. In the apparent victory of evil over God in Christ lies the *actual* victory of God over evil. The cross of Christ is the place where justice and mercy meet, where the justice of God opens the way for peace for men. The death of Christ proves that God is just and that he justifies him who has faith in Jesus (Rom.3:26); those who are justified by faith in Jesus have peace with God (Rom.5:1).

The problem for us arises in trying to use the cross as a model for political action. On the one hand (as some Christians have argued), the cross shows us God's willingness to go to any cost in the fight against evil, and to secure justice. On the other hand, as many pacifists argue, the cross shows us Jesus' way of responding to evil, namely by refusing to use force in return. The ambiguity here needs to be understood in the light of the Christian view of history which we began to look at in Chapter 6 in our discussion of the flood.

After the flood, fallen mankind is given a new 'creation' with a new task, but within the constraints of a fallen world order. We now need institutional structures which, though within God's permission, did not exist in the perfection of the Garden. We are now in a provisional age, the age between the fall and the Last Day. The life, death and resurrection of Christ are a decisive new event within this history. Here in him the New Age is beginning. In him the kingdom of God has come among us. In his cross there is promised freedom from the powers of evil, freedom from the tensions of the fallen world, healing for social divisions and personal disorder.

But though the kingdom has burst into the world in Christ and stands before us as a goal and a hope, in actual practical living the kingdom in its fulness is still to come, and the promise is yet to be completely fulfilled. 'Thy kingdom come, thy will be done in earth as it is in heaven.' There is peace in the cross, but the experience of peace will become complete reality only in the new heaven and the new earth in which righteousness dwells. There is a 'not yet' to our salvation, as well as a 'now'. This present time is the 'eschatological reserve' – the waiting for the fulness of the kingdom to come, while at the same time living within the constraints of the fallen world in its continuing disorder. This is the time between the decisive battle of the war and the final end to all mopping-up operations of enemy action.

Can there, then, be peace in our time?

Real peace between men and nations can only be the peace of God, the peace found in Christ. It is 'in him', as Ephesians reminds us, that dividing walls of hostility between even Jew and Gentile can be broken down, and that together they can affirm: 'He is our peace' (Eph.2:14). But until the kingdoms of this world become the kingdoms of our God and his Christ (*cf.* Rev.11:15), until there is established a social order 'in which righteousness dwells' (2 Pet.3:13), the peace of this world can never be the deep peace of Christ. It can at best be co-existence and the absence of hostilities. There is no deep peace within the structures of this world, although the Christian must move as far as possible towards establishing the justice on which peace depends, and to working for the limited peace of co-existence. But we cannot act as though the new age had already come in its fulness. We must rather live in the present in the light of the coming future. The day will come when there will be no more death, no more crying, no more tears. The former things will pass away, and all will be made new. Swords will one day be beaten into plough-shares and spears into pruning hooks. But for the present, while evil and injustice are still part of our experience, the Christian calling is to be faithful to Christ within the orders of this fallen world. That will mean taking seriously our calling to be peacemakers where and when we can. It will mean also taking seriously our Christian obligations of neighbour love which require action in the cause of justice. Both are important. Our quest for justice and for peace will also require us to work for such social institutions which most adequately serve the needs of people: we need institutions which serve the cause of justice and of peace. To what extent these two callings can be compatible with a call to arms, and if necessary to fight, is a matter for each individual Christian conscience.

This much, however, is certain. History has a direction. Rather than the question of fatalistic despair: 'What is the world coming to?', the Christian answers in terms of him to whom the world is coming – or even of him who is coming to his world. The victory of Christ is part of a wider purpose of God which, the writer to Ephesians affirms, God is now making known through his church, namely 'to unite all things in him [Christ], things in heaven and things on earth' (Eph.1:10).

This world, in other words, is sustained by God's providence. Its future is ultimately in his hands. The New Testament speaks of the day in which this world order is to cease as 'the coming of the day of God' (2 Pet.3:12), and this present age as a time of God's forbearance to give opportunity for repentance and faith (2 Pet.3:9). While this fact should encourage Christian people to 'wait for' his coming Day, to 'be zealous to be found by him without spot or blemish, and at peace' (2 Pet.3:12,14), it also draws the line between the decisions of Christian obedience (which are ours to take), and decisions concerning the ending of this world order (which belong within God's providence). When we come to discuss the possibilities of mutual annihilation and the ending of human society, brought closer by the existence of weapons of indiscriminate and massive destructive power, we shall need to keep closely in mind that God has called us to establish justice, and that the close of the age is a decision which belongs within his providence and his judgment alone. Let us remember, though, that the advent theme of the close of the age and the coming of the Lord is constantly addressed in the pages of the New Testament in terms of encouragement and hope:

'And when you hear of wars and tumults, do not be terrified; ... nation will rise against nation, and kingdom against kingdom ... when you see Jerusalem surrounded by armies, then know that its desolation has come near ... when these things begin to take place, look up and raise your heads, because your redemption is drawing near' (Lk.21:9–10,20,28).

Part 4 _____

Starting to build –
right, wrong, war and
nuclear deterrence

14 'Just war' in today's world?

We have now come to the point at which we can begin to see something of the ground-plan for a theological foundation on which to build some moral decisions. From such a perspective we could go back to the specific biblical examples and see how they belong within a wider theological framework. From such a perspective we could begin to evaluate the different viewpoints expressed by different Christians at different times. It is from such a starting-point that each of us must now come to our own judgment on the moral and consequent political questions raised for us in today's world. In this chapter, I want to tell you some of the moral conclusions to which I come. Inevitably there are places where you will not share my conclusions. I hope, though, that you will be able to decide more clearly on what theological grounds you hold the views you do, and by what criteria you decide where you agree with me and where you do not.

  I begin by underlining the divine command to respect and protect human life, the command summarized in the words, 'Thou shalt do no murder'. The whole created order is the scene for the calling out of humanness from the wide range of creatureliness to be the bearer of God's image. It is human life which is capable of expressing in interpersonal relationships something of the nature of God. It is human flesh which the Word became in the pivotal event of world history. It is human life which at the day of resurrection will be the voice of the universe in praise to the Creator, and in which all the rest of creation, now groaning in travail, will find its liberty. Human life is precious. It is to be respected and protected.

The structure of the state exists by divine permission precisely to preserve and protect life, and to facilitate the conditions under which life may be lived before the Creator. The Christian quest for justice is not to be understood as a quest for some abstract principle. It is a quest for the social expression of neighbour-love. Justice is *for people*, to bring individual and community life more into line with the character of God and with his will, which is our welfare. Justice is the prerequisite for true *shalom* peace.

On the other hand, the biblical analysis of human nature indicates that we are living in a world in which wickedness, if unrestrained, would be rampant and destructive. The state is given by God also to act as that restraint. It is a result of and remedy for the way individual self-interest coupled with aggression all too easily, and especially within groups, leads to injustice and disorder in societies and between communities. For there to be justice, there has to be order, and for there to be order, there has to be enforceable law, and for there to be enforcement, the law has to have teeth. From such a viewpoint it is hard to square the denial of the propriety of ever using force (as some absolute pacifists believe) with the biblical emphasis on the sinfulness of man, and the need for some ordering restraint. The existence of government with the right to punish evil and a duty to promote a context for good is part of God's 'common grace' – an 'alien' work of his love.

It is in the attempt to hold these theological emphases

together that many Christians have come to the view that some limited war can be justified as part of the restraining function of the state in defence against evil aggression. But it can only be justified as a justifiable exception to the otherwise universal command against taking human life. It depends on the view that there can be some limited killing which is not murder.

The 'just war' theory developed among Christian thinkers precisely as an attempt to give expression to the view that Christian love sometimes needs this 'alien' expression of enforced justice which may include a limited resort to war. As Paul Ramsey puts it,

> The limitation placed upon conduct in the just war theory arose not from autonomous natural reason asserting its sovereignty over determinations of right and wrong . . . but from a quite humble moral reason subjecting itself to the sovereignty of God and the lordship of Christ, as Christian men felt themselves impelled out of love to justify war, and by love severely to limit war.[1]

A just war can, then, only be a limited war. And the primary principle of limitation in the conduct of war, expressed variously by the 'just war' criteria of discrimination and proportion, is that non-combatants with a remote relationship to the conduct of the war should not be directly and intentionally killed. This is an attempt to give expression to the crucial moral distinction between justified killing and murder. From this standpoint, our first moral judgment about war, therefore, must be a critique of the crusader mentality which fails to see that war can only be justified as an exception to the law against murder, and that for war to be just it must be severely limited.

Critique of militarism

I believe that Barth's emphasis is correct when he affirms that, even if we are not persuaded of the rightness of an absolute pacifist line, the Christian church's first words must be those of keeping alive the enormity and abnormality and horror of war, and acting as a restraint against the sort of militarist thinking which seeks some sort of justification for waging it without regard to moral bounds. One duty of Christian ethics in this area is to recover the ground on which to offer a critique of bellicose militarism. War may not be thought of as a proper and normal function of the state, or as an inevitable part of the state's duties. The church must remind the state that the exercise of its powers in this area must be seen as abnormal. It must remind that state that mass slaughter may very well be mass murder. It must insist that the state may not initiate aggressive action in threatening attack on another. The possibility of war may only be seized, as Barth put it, 'at the very last hour and in the darkest of days'.[2]

Bernard Häring comments: 'One of the greatest threats to the survival of humankind and of cohumanity in our time, is the secularised form of the "holy war" tradition.' The Second Vatican Council refers to 'unbending ideologies' among which, says Häring, we must include not only extreme communism, but also those 'no less fanatical anti-communists who in a kind of "holy war" rage would be willing to use the whole arsenal of weapons which can exterminate humankind many times over.'[3] As Christians we must work for the utter removal of this 'crusading' tradition.

In this context, much of the chauvinistic reaction from parts of the British press and public to the despatch of the Task Force to the Falklands in 1982 appears in the cold light of day to smack of precisely that tradition. How much of the decision to send the Task Force was the reaction of a wounded national pride, how much a calculated military judgment that if force was going to have to be used, then it would need to be immediate, and how much the tragic last resort after all diplomacy had failed?

It is only when a state can no longer by other means maintain a context of justice in which life can be protected and a just order of life preserved, that sooner or later it may, as an utter last resort, be compelled to take up arms, or inflict that abnormal task on another state. 'The first, and basic and decisive point which Christian ethics must make in this matter is that the state – the totality of responsible citizens – and each individual in his own conduct – should so fashion peace while there is still time that it will not lead to this explosion, but make war superfluous.'[4]

In other words, ways must be found of providing institutions for peace, and of maintaining conventions in the restraints of power. The primary moral issue in this area is neither rearmament nor disarmament: it is the restoration and maintenance of an order of life – and of the institutions of dialogue and negotiation, and the structures of restraint in the exercise of human power, which will support and encourage it – in which life is meaningful and just, and in which individual personal choices are significant.

On the one hand, we must refuse the notion that wickedness can simply be talked away. We must have institutions capable of enforcing order. On the other hand, we must reject the notion of historical necessity. Wars do not just happen. It is people who decide to go to war. It is people who can negotiate conventions of restraint even in the face of nuclear accident or terrorist blackmail.

The Christian further acknowledges that neither nations nor institutions have any absolute existence. They have only a provisional and limited role under God. There may, therefore, even be circumstances in which it could be right to surrender a particular form of the state for the sake of avoiding mass murder.

Only when all this has been said, am I able to agree that pacifism is not possible. To follow Barth once more:

The conduct of one state or nation can throw another into the wholly abnormal situation of emergency in which not merely its greater or lesser prosperity but its very existence and autonomy are menaced and attacked. In consequence of this attitude of this other state, a nation can find itself faced by the question whether it must surrender or assert itself as such in the face of the claims of the other. Nothing less than this final question must be at issue if a war is to be just and necessary.[5]

It may be that in and with the independence of a nation are bound up certain values which Christians believe they hold in trust for God and must not surrender. In our day it could be that Christians in the West might have to face the threat of an aggressive communist attempt to impose an atheistic ideology. The choice would have to be faced as to the means by which such a threat should be answered. It may be that a nation is bound by treaty to another nation whose own security, and whose values held in trust for God, are threatened. A nation may be obliged to stand for truth and justice in the face of an aggressor who threatens these values. 'If Christian ethics has said all that there is to be said about true peace and the practical avoidability of war; if it has honestly and resolutely opposed a radical militarism; it may then add that, should the command of God require a nation to defend itself in such an emergency, or in solidarity with another nation in such an emergency, then it not only may but must do so.'[6]

Sometimes, in other words, in a situation of direct emergency, in which the preservation of human society in order and justice is being severely threatened (which perhaps gives content to Barth's elusive phrase about the 'command' of God'), then I believe Christian ethics can acknowledge the necessity of defensive, limited war as a last resort. This sort of war is not about national honour or state sovereignty; it is not about wounded pride or territorial expansion; it is about holding in trust for God a certain just order and the institutions which preserve and protect life and which otherwise would be lost. It is about the priority of justice: the political expression of neighbour love.

The difficulties of deciding when that 'last resort' is

reached – and indeed the difference between a *moral* last resort, and the political judgment as to *when* resort to force be undertaken – are well illustrated in the case of the Falklands War between Britain and Argentina. Some Christians took the view that since sovereign territory had been aggressively taken by force, force was needed to remove the aggressor. The question as to *when* that force should be used was one of political and military judgment. Justice is vindicated, they argued, when aggression is not allowed to succeed.

Other Christians believed that the immediate resort to force by the British Government was disproportionate and exacerbated the size of the conflict. If Britain had not been trying to negotiate over the future of the Islands for seventeen years, they argued; if she had tried all conceivable means of diplomatic response to the Argentine invasion; if she had forced and enforced economic and diplomatic sanctions; if in the utter last resort there had been no other way, then might the sending of the Task Force have been justified and the deaths of 1,000 human beings in that conflict have had some point.

The 'borderline' nature of war

No issues illustrate more pointedly than war, and the moral dilemmas associated with the conduct of modern war, what Helmut Thielicke called 'the ethical borderline'. In the fallen world ethical decision-making is not simply or straightforwardly a matter of applying a moral principle to a clear-cut situation. Christian moral decision-making is usually about the conflict of principles, weighing the relevance of certain facts, weighing the moral values at stake in the issue, giving some weighting to these values in order to judge between greater goods and lesser evils, assessing the consequences of any possible options, and coming to a decision in the situation whereby allegiance to God may best be expressed. When considering the problem of warfare, where questions have to be faced concerning the taking of life for the sake of preserving an order in which life can be lived, the process of moral judgment is by no means straightforward, and it may be that, because of human sin and the disorders of the fallen world, there are no ways open to us which are 'good'.

In his book *Not Only Peace* Alan Booth asks, 'How much injustice is it tolerable to connive at, rather than risk the outbreak of violence on an international scale?'[7] He then comments on the general tendency of contemporary moralists to emphasize the over-riding evil of war itself, particularly in view of the possibilities of escalation, so that if violence breaks out, other aspects of the problem may be put aside in favour of appeals to cease fire. This choice, however, may be only one of several choices open. 'In practice we find that a serious attempt to reach a sound moral appreciation of the great issues between the nations always involves us in an attempt to balance competing considerations so that we have no process of slide-rule certainty for reaching a decision.'[8]

Furthermore, of course, in international conflicts moral aspects are inextricably interwoven with technical ones. There are competing moral claims to be met. Politics, the art of the possible, operates in the area of such competing claims and, inevitably, of unavoidable compromise.

It is at this point that Thielicke's discussion of the borderline is so crucial. As we saw, sometimes there is no way open to us without incurring the guilt of doing evil. In theological terms, this is part of the reality of the fallen world. Our task is to understand the questions as best we can from a theological perspective, and formulate policies of action which, as far as possible, maximize the movement towards justice, order and peace. In the course of the task, it may be that there are no ways open to us which do not involve some measure of guilt – of getting our hands dirty in the disorder of the fallen world. The Christian who engages in war may do so, it seems to me, only under the rubric of penitence and the assurance of forgiveness. And he is assured of that forgiveness when, as far as is open to him, his moral choices have been made in the conscious desire to express allegiance to his Lord, and in the light of the moral truths of God's character which he has revealed.

That is, of course, very far from saying that 'anything goes'. There are moral boundary conditions which set limits beyond which any action is morally inadmissible. It was precisely to set such boundaries that the 'just war' theory was developed. We need now to explore how this could be of help in today's world.

A 'just war' in today's world?

Even if the theoretical question of the justice of some causes for war is agreed, there still remains the pressing practical problem of whether, in the world of modern technological weapons, it could be possible for war to be conducted justly within the terms of the 'just war' tradition.

Bernard Häring writes: 'After all the experiences through which history teaches us, and in view of the deadly arsenal of weapons that can destroy humankind and poison the whole ecological system, it should be clear, that even on its own reasoning, the traditional 'just war' theory can no longer be applied.'[9] This, however, passes too quickly over some important distinctions. We need to be clear about our method of reaching moral judgments, for morality is not only about assessing the consequences of certain actions, but also about the congruence of those actions with principles of action which embody neighbour love. Love distinguishes between certain actions which are permitted and certain actions which are prohibited, and these distinctions are not based wholly on assessing consequences and weighing risk.

In this particular case, we need to try to distinguish between the *moral* question of the justice of means used in waging war, and the quite separate question of the *risk* of certain consequences which those means may entail. It is only when the questions of moral principle and conflicting *moral* claims have been clarified, setting moral boundaries to action, that the assessment of the *risk* of consequences becomes important. This is another way of asking whether,

183

in today's world, the moral criteria of the 'just war' tradition can still have some validity.

I would argue that for any war to be just, and to be fought justly, it has at least to be limited by the moral boundary expressed in the principle of non-combatant immunity. By such a limitation, some recognition can be taken of the biblical distinction between killing in war and the 'shedding of innocent blood', and therefore between justified, limited war and murder. Murder, in other words, sets limits to war.

Of course in modern warfare the lines between combatants and non-combatants are difficult to draw. In *some* sense everyone in modern war is a 'military person'. None can escape some involvement in the war effort, nor in the effects of the war. The tank commander at the front needs the stores officer way back behind the front line; he needs the munitions made in factories; he needs food, drink and uniform. Is the worker in the factory which makes the uniform any less involved than the tank commander who wears it? To be sure, the lines are blurred, and, as Lord Cranborne's reply to Bishop Bell in 1944 indicated, the definition of 'military target' is not unambiguous either (should centres of war administration be called 'military'?). However, despite the blurred lines, discrimination must still be made between combatants who are directly engaged in the conduct of the war, and non-combatants whose relation to the conduct of the war is more distant. And here, the 'just war' criterion of proportion becomes important. This criterion requires that *no more force than is necessary* be used to achieve an objective. There are other ways of confronting a worker in a uniform factory than killing him. There may be no other ways of confronting the commander of a tank.

On this criterion, the obliteration bombing of the centres of predominantly civilian population cannot be justified, even for the sake of military targets contained within them. Just as it can never be a moral act to kill an aggressor's children in order to deter his aggression – which would be to respond to unjust aggression by an unjust and arbitrary taking of innocent life – so neither can it be a moral act deliberately and directly to kill non-combatants as a means of combating the aggressive intent of others. To quote Ramsey again: 'We do not need to know *who* and *where* the non-combatants are in order to know that indiscriminate bombing exceeds the moral limits of warfare that can ever barely be justified. We have only to know that there *are* non-combatants – even only the children, the sick and the aged – in order to know the basic moral difference between limited and total war.' Then, in response to the view that it is now practically impossible to distinguish between 'guilty' and 'innocent' in a modern war, Ramsey continues, 'Whoever clothed non-combatants with moral immunity from direct attack by assessing their personal innocence? In the past "guilt" has meant close relation to or direct participation in the conduct of war (or with the force which should be repelled): and "innocence", the relation or non-relation to this.'[10]

The 'just war' principle of non-combatant immunity expressed in the criteria of discrimination and proportion can thus be seen to have continuing and crucial validity in the conduct of modern war. If weapons can be targetted discriminately, if the force used is the minimum necessary to achieve the goal of immobilizing the aggressor, if targetting intentions can distinguish between combatants and non-combatants (recognizing the inevitable accidental loss of non-combatant life), then as a last resort defensive action against unjust aggression – limited war – can be justified.

In this context we must consider the view that counterforce tactical (battlefield) nuclear weapons could be thought to be similar to conventional weapons in their ability to fulfil these criteria of discrimination and proportion. In terms of moral principle, it seems to me that if such a weapon could be targetted accurately onto a military target, or used as a warning shot over uninhabited territory, then subject to the four caveats below, the use of such a weapon might be no more immoral than a conventional attack on the same target. But the caveats are crucially important.

The first concerns the criterion of proportion, and the question would need to be asked whether there was in fact no other way through conventional means of obtaining the desired resistance to enemy aggression. The second concerns the indiscriminate ecological and personal damage which would be caused by radiation. Suppose an aggressive army of enemy volunteers were advancing through uninhabited and uninhabitable desert, it might just be that a tactical nuclear strike could be thought the only way of restraining them, and such a limited strike might then be considered no more immoral than a series of conventional strikes. However, it is very hard to see how such a strike could ever be defended as indiscriminate were it to be undertaken, for example, on the 'battlefield' of Europe.

Thirdly, at this point the element of risk becomes crucial. For *at present* there is persuasive argument from some military thinkers (such as Lord Mountbatten and Lord Carver) who fail to find the possibility of limited tactical nuclear strike at all credible, and see the likelihood of escalation into total strategic exchange as virtually certain. Once the nuclear firebreak is crossed, the consequences of escalation are unpredictable. On these three grounds, therefore, although theoretically a limited tactical nuclear strike could be judged no less immoral than certain sorts of discriminate conventional attack, *in practice at present* it seems to me very close to the borders of immorality.

There is a fourth caveat to be made. This concerns the message that is given to a potential aggressor by our possession of and willingness to use a tactical nuclear weapon. Within the terms of the criteria we have been discussing, it needs to be unmistakably clear that our intentions are wholly defensive and not at all aggressive. The *sorts* of weapons being held need to be assessed according to such criteria. Both the ground-launched Cruise missile, with a range of over 1,500 miles, and Pershing II ballistic missiles with first-strike characteristics come within the Theatre Nuclear Force modernization programme, and both are clearly perceived as 'war-fighting' weapons. They are not unambiguously weapons of defence and deterrence. The message being given is that NATO is ready to use such weapons on a European battlefield. Is this any longer primarily 'deterrence', or is it more definitely 'readiness for war'?

Indiscriminate weapons

When we come to weapons which are indiscriminate by design (whether they be strategic nuclear weapons, or chemical or biological weapons), or to the designedly indiscriminate use of conventional weapons (as in obliteration bombing of predominantly civilian populations), the moral situation is very clear. The answer of Christian morality must be an unqualified 'no'. Let us look at various possible uses of strategic nuclear weapons, and see why in each case this must be so.

Strategic nuclear weapons could be used in three possible ways: aggressively, in a first strike; defensively, in a first strike in response to conventional attack from an enemy; and in a retaliatory second strike in response to their use by an enemy. From all we have said, it is clear that aggressive war *per se* must be judged immoral, and that therefore no aggressive first use of nuclear weapons could ever be justified. A *defensive* first strike must also be judged immoral on the grounds of its necessarily indiscriminate nature. Any weapon which is designed for the purpose of directly killing non-combatants as a means of achieving some military advantage, even though it may also hit some military targets, is a weapon whose every use would be immoral. It is in that sense that we might describe such weapons as are indiscriminate *by design* as intrinsically immoral weapons.

There is a further reason also. If, as seems inevitable, the use of strategic nuclear weapons would involve mutual exchange of weapons of indiscriminate and devastating destructive power, then the possibility of such weapons being used 'in defence' becomes remote. For mutual annihilation is not defence, it is suicide. And if defence becomes identical with the obliteration of the societies for which the defence is undertaken, we have reached an absurdity as well as extreme immorality. As Archbishop Runcie said: 'There can be no such thing as just mutual obliteration.' Or, to quote again some words from Thielicke,

> The concept of a just war, i.e. a war of defence, is meaningful only so long as defence is possible. This means that there has to be some chance of survival, and some reasonable relation between the destruction to be inflicted and the good to be defended. But if in the case of atomic powers of approximately equal strength both attack and defence come increasingly to be identical with self-annihilation, then these distinctions fall to the ground, and the whole concept of a just war becomes absurd.[11]

There is yet a third line of argument which is important. The command of God given in the Noachic covenant was that life should be preserved, and that the means used should be the means of justice. God, in other words, requires that social order shall be preserved and protected. It is by God's decree that this world order is upheld and maintained. It is in his prerogative when this world order shall cease. For man to take decisions which will bring to its close this world order and the possibility of the preservation of human life at all, is for man to play God. Our human task is the stewardship of this world, and the provision of a context in which life may be lived. It is not given to us to decide when this world shall cease. For men to take that sort of decision into their own hands is to exceed their God-given tasks, and to succumb to the demonic.

Second strike
Suppose we agree that a first strike nuclear attack is not an option open for Christian morality in any circumstances. Suppose, for the sake of argument at this stage, that strategic nuclear weapons have been kept for the purposes of deter-

ring a first strike from the enemy. (In a later section we will look at the morality of deterrence much more fully.) Suppose, now, that deterrence has failed. Is a second strike any morally different from a first?

The illustration is sometimes given of the terrorist holding hostage a class of schoolchildren, threatening to kill them if his demands are not met. In response, and in order to deter his action, government officials take hostage the terrorist's own children and threaten to kill them if the terrorist does kill his hostages. Suppose, now, that deterrence has failed: the gunman has killed the schoolchildren. The question is: should the government officials carry out their threat of what now amounts to bare retaliation? Could such retaliation ever be morally justified?

In this example (even if we conceded that it could be moral for the government officials to take the terrorist's children hostage at all – which is very questionable), the moral situation is very different once the deterrent has failed. The cause which gave rise to the threat (the safety of the schoolchildren) no longer obtains. Can there be any other moral reason for retaliation?

In terms of a second strike nuclear retaliation, the only justification that could be offered would be in terms of punishment. It could be put this way: Might not a nation engaging in the immoral first use of nuclear weapons *deserve* the retributive response of a retaliatory strike, even though a first strike against that nation would be inexcusable? To this it must be replied, however, that the same criteria of discrimination and proportion which make the first strike morally inadmissible still obtain. And furthermore, to 'punish' by means of nuclear weapons with their indiscriminate effect would be to punish the innocent (non-combatant) massively, not just the guilty; it would be punishing the innocent for the guilt of the guilty; and the less guilty would be punished as if they were the most guilty. And this would be blatantly unjust and murderous.

Furthermore, to recall our earlier discussion, the whole

rationale for the principle of retributive justice in any case depends on the maintenance of the created order under the rubric of the Noachic covenant. That is what justice is about. To 'punish' by obliterating the social order by which justice is defined, is to talk not about punishment, but about annihilation. Furthermore, *even if* all the victims fully deserved such a massive punishment, that exercise of 'vengeance' belongs to God and not to us. To engage in a second strike, therefore, would be to take to ourselves the right to pronounce ultimate vengeance, which properly can only belong to God himself. A retaliatory second strike could not, therefore, even be justified on grounds of 'punishment'.

We conclude that there are no circumstances ever in which it could be morally justifiable to use indiscriminate strategic nuclear weapons. As the doctors (for other reasons) wrote in *The Medical Consequences of Nuclear Weapons*, 'Nuclear warfare must never be allowed to happen.'[12] No-one could justify pushing the nuclear button, no matter who pushes it, or for what reason.[13]

Notes for chapter fourteen

[1]P. Ramsey, *War and the Christian Conscience* (Duke University Press, 1961), p.59.

[2]K. Barth, *Church Dogmatics*, **3** (4) (English Translation, T. & T. Clark, 1955), pp.450ff.

[3]B. Häring, *Free and Faithful in Christ*, **3** (St Paul Publications, 1981), p.404.

[4]K. Barth, *op.cit.*, p.459.

[5]*Ibid.*, p.461.

[6]*Ibid.*, p.462.

[7]Alan Booth, *Not Only Peace* (SCM, 1967), p.41.

[8]*Ibid.*, p.41.

[9]B. Häring, *op.cit.*, p.407.

[10]P. Ramsey, *op.cit.*, p.144.

[11]H. Thielicke, *Theological Ethics*, **2** (English Translation, Eerdmans, 1969), p.474.

[12]*The Medical Consequences of Nuclear Weapons* (Medical Campaign Against Nuclear Weapons, 1982).

[13]*Cf.* L. Smedes in *Mere Morality* (Eerdmans, 1983), p.270.

15 The problems of nuclear deterrence

We must now explore the complex questions raised by the brute fact that the world does now have horrific and growing arsenals of strategic nuclear weapons, the use of which – we have argued – would be both morally wrong and utter folly, and look at the reliance that so many political leaders have been placing on the concept of nuclear deterrence. We will concentrate our attention on strategic weapons which are indiscriminate and disproportionate by design, acknowledging that, while any use of such weapons is morally outlawed, there could be a *moral* case for the use of tactical, discriminate nuclear weapons on specifically defined military targets; though, as we have said, the problems of *risk* of escalation are probably such as to outlaw their use also. Our task in this chapter is to examine the arguments for and against keeping strategic nuclear weapons as a deterrent, and to explore whether nuclear deterrence is the least morally compromised way of averting a nuclear holocaust.

There is nothing new about the concept of deterrence itself. Police forces, disciplinary procedures and so on are forms of deterrence to restrain possible evil. Part of the reference in Romans 13:3–5 to the magistrate's sword is to its deterrent effect: 'Would you have no fear of him who is in authority? Then do what is good . . .'. However, there can be moral and immoral deterrents. The question at issue in the case of nuclear weapons is whether their use as a deterrent is moral or immoral, or perhaps less immoral than any alternative.

We will look first at some of the practical effects of reliance on nuclear deterrence in recent years. Then we will come to the moral questions and examine arguments for and against the concept of nuclear deterrence.

The practical realities

First, some form of deterrent becomes necessary once it is agreed that man is basically given up to mistrust. We live in a world in which potential aggression could well become actual aggression if unrestrained and undeterred. In the context of East/West confrontation since World War II, in practice nuclear deterrence has often not merely tended to respond to the fact of basic mistrust, but has sometimes also fostered that mistrust by maximizing the sense in which the other 'side' is perceived as 'threat'. The Christian in the West has to make a judgment about the sort of threat which the Warsaw Pact forces, and the political leaderships behind them, actually pose to the West. Are we seeing the Soviet Union reacting to threats to its own borders, and needing to maintain its buffer states, or are we – as many of the war games scenarios seem to suggest – witnessing preparations for Soviet aggressive action against the West? If the latter, we need then to ask to what extent Soviet aggression, and the attempt to impose a militantly atheistic ideological system, is facing the West with what Thielicke calls 'the ethical borderline', in which the Christian may be called on to use evil means in the fight against an evil ideology.

Second, deterrence assumes a rationality in those who are in a position to decide on the use of weapons. Deterrence is based on rational calculations of threat or bluff, and on the assumption that those in power will not do utterly irrational and utterly erratic things. The opponent, it is assumed, is in a position to assess the cost to himself and cares enough about that to avoid inviting an unacceptably damaging response to his aggression.

Third, deterrence requires such escalation as is necessary for the deterrent to remain effective. As Churchill hinted, the worse the weapons can possibly be, the more likely it is that aggression will be deterred. If it is true that 'no responsible statesman, concerned with the protection of the citizens who have elected him to office, can afford to leave his country without a nuclear guarantee'[1], then escalation seems built in to deterrence. And not only escalation: proliferation is also built in, as increasing numbers of countries will feel obliged to join the 'nuclear club'.

Fourth, deterrence seems in practice to have led to a self-perpetuating spiral of escalation. While this is not a necessary consequence of nuclear deterrence in theory, in practice, despite the SALT talks and the glimmers of hope in the START negotiations, the escalating spiral of arms build-up continues. The political need for a strong bargaining position at the negotiating table requires that one's weapons remain effective deterrents. Furthermore, the separate pressures of economic, military, political, diplomatic and technological concerns all force the spiral upwards. None moves it downwards. There seems also frequently to be a tendency in such a complex of concerns towards lack of responsibility for the spiral. Power is invested in the system itself. Deterrence – at least in some people's minds – leads to a built-in fatalism and refusal of personal responsibility.

Fifth, deterrence as practised has often assumed that security is increased and defence improved if numbers of weapons are increased. There is an assumption that increasing warheads necessarily increases deterrence. The truth might be that rather than reducing risk, the risks are increased.

Sixth, deterrence can foster the notion of bare power. While there have been leaders who sought to maximize détente while keeping a nuclear deterrent guarantee, there have been others whose determination to match strength with strength has been affirmed even when the question 'For what are we standing firm?' has apparently ceased to be asked.

Seventh, nuclear deterrence in practice so far has involved a deliberate and serious threat of massive retaliation. Whatever the other side can do to us, we must make it clear that we can make it unacceptably bad for them.

Finally, deterrence depends on a confusion between capabilities and intentions. Because one side has a certain capability, the assumption is fostered that it is intending to use it. This also necessarily cuts two ways. Because the West can measure Soviet capabilities, for example, it believes that it can then make a certain judgment about Soviet intentions. And, by the nature of strategic thinking and the need to prepare for the worst, the assumption can be fostered that the Soviet Union *intends* the worst. And this works precisely the other way also. The only measure the East has of Western intentions is its measure of Western capabilities. Deterrence depends on an uncertainty as to how far the other side would be prepared to go in using the capability it possesses. We will come back to this point later in our discussion.

Such, it seems to me, are some of the practical realities of the way nuclear deterrence is working. Some of these practical results of deterrence are not necessarily implied by deterrence theory, and may come about through other factors, political or otherwise. Some are more morally dubious than others. The Christian is then faced with a series of questions. In the first place, what assessment is he or she to make of the morality of nuclear deterrence both in terms of possibilities and in terms of actual political realities, and then what actions should that lead him or her to adopt in terms of seeking to change the political realities if necessary?

The moral arguments

The moral case in favour of nuclear deterrence begins with an acknowledgment of the fact that we are in a world in which such weapons exist, and that the knowledge for their construction (as far as we can see) will for ever be available. In such a context, could it be morally defensible for us as a nation to abandon possession of them? To do so would mean, as Bishop Leonard puts it, that 'for all time, the power to exercise authority would in the last resort be with those who had no inhibition about their use'.[2] In other words, states with no nuclear guarantee (of their own or their allies) would be open to nuclear blackmail from any potential aggressor state or unscrupulous dictator who had access to such weapons.

One of the most detailed Christian assessments of the theory of nuclear deterrence comes from the pen of Helmut

Thielicke. He begins with two facts: one is the existence of nuclear weapons, the other is the untrustworthiness of the men who are capable of using them. The question of the avoidance of nuclear war, therefore, is not only a matter of getting rid of weapons. It is also an attempt to cope with mutual mistrust, based on inherent untrustworthiness, between potential aggressors. The theological grounds for the disarmament/deterrence dilemma is that 'fallen human existence is given up to mistrust'.

One of the primary problems in the possession of nuclear weapons is therefore not merely a matter of stated policies and strategies. It is also uncertainty about the other side's trustworthiness. Thielicke clarifies this with an illustration. Imagine, he says, two mortal enemies who suddenly meet in a room with cocked pistols in hand. Because the situation is equally dangerous to both, they agree that at the count of 'three' they will both throw their pistols out of the window. The count begins, but the word 'three' finds both pistols still in hand. For each believes that the other, in spite of the agreement, will not throw away his pistol, and will thus be in a position of superiority. Basic mistrust leads to each retaining their weapon while actually agreeing to renounce them. It is the serious theological grounds for the dilemma – the fallenness of man in a fallen world – which leads Thielicke to say that unless basic human untrustworthiness can be dealt with, then treaties and agreements are of doubtful value on their own.

In democratic societies, one way of coping with basic mistrust is in the 'distribution of powers', and in the resulting balance of power between different groups. What we now see in the East/West confrontation is an attempt on a much larger scale to achieve a 'balance of power' – this is the basis for an 'atomic peace'. But, as Thielicke says, the analogy with democratic states is not adequate. 'Atomic peace is illusory in the first place because, although it can make possible a temporary state of relative security, it can do so only by carrying with it a serious threat and hence also the possibility of atomic conflict. For if the resolve to use the atomic weapons even at the risk of one's own destruction is lacking, the weapons seem to lose their psychological effect and hence can no longer impose an atomic peace.'[3]

But if an atomic peace – which is surely very far from the peace of Christ – can be preserved only by a resolve to engage if necessary in nuclear war, then again we reach the borders of absurdity and immorality. 'If the mistrust in the world . . . can only be remedied by a balance of power, then such a remedy, grounded in the Noachic covenant, can be taken seriously by Christians only if it offers genuine possibilities of punishment, resistance, deterrence and defence.'[4] For these functions are only meaningful within a divinely willed preservation of the world. They are not compatible with a readiness for mutual annihilation, let alone the immorality of 'inhuman atrocity towards countless hosts of combatants and non-combatants alike'.[5]

Does the deterrent effect of nuclear weapons depend upon an intention to use them? There are four sorts of response to this question which we must examine in turn. These are: first, a genuine threat to use; second, bluff; third, possession with real uncertainty about use; and fourth, mere possession with no intention to use. (Thielicke's own view is a version of the fourth.)

The morality of a genuine threat to use nuclear weapons

For such a threat to be credible to a potential aggressor he must be sufficiently uncertain as to whether or not we are willing in some circumstances actually to use nuclear weapons. The view we are examining here is that deterrence works on the theory that to threaten to engage in a nuclear war is the safest way to avoid it ever happening, and that for the threat to be credible it has to be a *genuine* threat to use. But if, as we have argued, all such use of strategic nuclear weapons is morally forbidden, is not the threat itself also morally forbidden? Is not the genuine *intention to use* nuclear weapons as immoral as their actual use?

One way of handling this question has been proposed by Michael Novak, himself a firm believer in deterrence. He examines the moral paradox at the heart of nuclear deterrence thus:

> It is clear that the complexities of nuclear deterrence change the meaning of 'intention' and 'threat' as these words are usually used in moral discourse. Those who intend to prevent the use of nuclear weapons by maintaining a system of deterrence in readiness for use do *intend* to use such weapons, but only in order *not* to use them, and do *threaten* to use them, but only in order to *deter* their use. That this is no mere rationalisation is shown by the fact that several generations of nuclear weapons systems have become obsolete and retired without ever having been used. These are considered to be successful and moral systems. In the same way deterrence is judged to be successful in so far as nuclear war does not occur.[6]

Now this seems to be based either on an absurdity – that 'use' is the same as 'non-use' – or it involves an equivocation on the word 'use', so that 'use' sometimes means 'keep the weapons sitting in their silos', and sometimes, 'fire the weapons'. Either way Novak seems at this point to be playing with words.

Novak then tries to unpack the variety of meanings carried by the word 'intention'. In the carrying of a firearm, he suggests, a policeman, a burglar and a murderer have different intentions with respect to its use. The policeman *intends deterrence* and no actual use (unless governed by the requirement of justice and the disciplines of his profession); the burglar intends only a *threatening and conditional use outside justice*; the murderer intends *not a conditional but a wilful use*. In the case of nuclear deterrence, argues Novak, the intention is like the first, but not the second or third. However, we must reply that Novak's parenthesis also leads to the breakdown of his analogy. There *can* be a moral use for the policeman, and it is on this basis that his carrying of the firearm acts as a deterrent. But the question at issue is whether there can be a moral deterrent involved in an intention to do an *immoral* act (of using a nuclear weapon).

However, let us follow Novak a little further as he makes some distinctions: 'In nuclear matters we would further distinguish between a *fundamental*, *secondary* and *architectonic* intention. ... The *fundamental* moral intention in nuclear deterrence is never to have to use the deterrent force . . .'. He goes on:

> Deterrence requires by its nature a *secondary* intention. For the physical material weapon is by itself no deterrent without the engagement of intellect and will on the part of the entire public that called it into being. It is also no deterrent if it fails to meet and to halt the will, intellect and social organisation of the particular opposing regime. A people that would be judged incapable of willing to use the deterrent would tempt an adversary to call its bluff. Thus secondary intention cannot be separated from deterrence. Without that secondary intention, distinct from the fundamental intention, a deterrent is no longer a deterrent, but only an inert weapon backed up by a public lie . . .[7]

Novak then describes thirdly an *objective* intention, which he calls 'architectonic intention' – the political intention which suffuses the whole structure of the society committed to deterrence. At this level, the whole political machinery is geared to the intention to use the weapon.

> A society that possesses a deterrent also has an organised objective intention. In the case of the United States, individuals add to this objective intention subjective intentions which are both fundamental – that the deterrent succeed in never being used – and secondary – that the deterrent be held in readiness for use. The proposition that a nation may possess a deterrent but may not intend to

use it is fulfilled by the fundamental intention but not by the objective intention and the secondary intention. To condemn the latter is to frustrate the former and to invite a host of greater evils.[8]

In other words, in order to avert these 'greater evils' a nation has to intend (in an objective political, and a subjective personal sense) to do its own 'great evil', so that in fact it never happens (which is what it *fundamentally* intends).

What Novak never makes clear is how a person can be committed to the secondary and objective intentions sufficiently wholeheartedly for them to make sense, while also holding on to his fundamental intention – which is utterly opposite. Nor does he say (apart from the fact that this will avert greater evils) how a commitment to an evil secondary intention can somehow be justified by a morally praiseworthy fundamental intention.

There seems needless confusion here. Let us start with Novak's secondary intention, which is the intention actually to use nuclear weapons in certain circumstances. We have to ask: Is *that* intention morally justifiable? *Could* actual use be morally justified in those circumstances? Now if – as we have argued before – the answer to that question must be 'no' whatever the circumstances, then that secondary intention is immoral.

Once that is agreed, the only further question between the 'fundamental intention' and this evil 'secondary intention' reduces to a question of means and ends. Novak's thesis boils down to the view that the thing fundamentally intended is achieved only by the use of means (*i.e.* the *secondary* and *architectonic* intentions) which are themselves evil. And can the good end justify immoral means? Surely not.

Novak's argument seems to work by making one intention depend on another. If in fact it is seen to be simply a question of means and ends (complicated by the fact that one of the means is itself an 'intention'), then the only question to ask is: 'What *ought* we to intend?' Can it be moral at *any* level of

199

intention to threaten genocide and ecological holocaust?

If the threat to use nuclear weapons is a genuine threat, then it seems to me to be as immoral as the use itself.

The morality of bluff

The second consideration is the possibility of bluff. One course of action might be for a government to possess nuclear weapons but to have a firm intention never, whatever the circumstances, to use them, and to ensure that sufficient of the chain of military command know that the weapons must never be used. On that basis, for deterrence to be effective the government would then have to lie utterly convincingly so that all potential aggressors were given to understand that the possession of weapons was not bluff, but was a threat actually to use. The moral justification for such a view could be that in the 'ethical borderline' the immorality of lying could be considered less morally questionable than the immorality of using nuclear weapons, and it might be judged that such a course of bluff plus lies is the only way of averting their actual use. The moral question here is the extent to which we may get our hands dirty in this fallen world, in order to make for the least morally compromised outcome.

In reply to this suggestion, it could be argued that, even if the Cabinet and high military command were 'in on' the bluff, the necessarily and essentially secret nature of the bluff would mean that others were *required* to believe in the intention to use, and indeed be prepared to use if necessary. As Roger Ruston puts it: 'If we agree to the possession of the deterrent by our country, we may not thereby morally absent ourselves from the individuals (the thousands of people who are trained in maintenance and firing routines, the strategic planners and commanders) who are fully prepared to use it when the occasion arises.'[9] Furthermore, the government could not let on the nature of the bluff to its electorate. It would have to be elected on a lie. And the lie would have to be sufficiently wholeheartedly believed by the nation for it also to be seriously believed by any potential aggressor.

There are several moral dilemmas involved here. The first is the extent to which it could become excusable, in this fallen world, for a democratically elected government to depart from the principles of justice before its electorate by engaging in widespread public deceit, for the sake of the just cause of preventing a nuclear war, and for the protection of a society within which justice is possible. Such a politics of deceit would seem very far from the justice for which the exercise is undertaken.

Secondly, for the deceit to be believed sufficiently widely for deterrence to be effective, the government would be requiring the majority of the nation actually to intend to use and to prepare to use nuclear weapons, even though they knew (but the people did not) that the weapons would not be used. In other words, although the leaders might be cleared of the charge of the immoral intention to use nuclear weapons, in favour of the charge of fostering widespread deceit, the nation as a whole would be required to have this immoral intention, which as we discussed earlier is morally unacceptable.

Thirdly, even though the policy be bluff in the last analysis, to engage in such a bluff would seem to require an abandonment of the quest for justice in international politics. A *just* deterrent can be mounted only by the resolve of a nation to act decisively and rationally to maintain justice. But (as O'Donovan argues), in order to deter one's enemies with nuclear weapons, it is no longer a matter of convincing them that we care about justice – it is a matter of convincing them that we are foolishly reckless and very dangerous when provoked. The intention to use nuclear weapons (even when bluff) is a 'deliberate conjuring with the morally unthinkable in order to impress one's enemies'.[10]

So if an intention to use nuclear weapons, even for the sake of deterring their use, is immoral, and if a policy of bluff and thus widespread deceit, even if likely to work, is effectively a statement that justice doesn't matter, does this not mean that the only course open for a Christian is to argue for the unilateral renunciation of nuclear weapons? Both these considerations seem to point powerfully in this direction. However, there are two other possible courses open.

Keep the weapons, but remain unsure about use

To judge from the comments of some politicians, it could well be that leaders of nuclear powers believe it right to retain nuclear weapons, but *simply do not know* whether they would use them in a crisis. This position avoids the moral condemnation we have made of threats and of bluff. It does, however, still make the effectiveness of deterrence depend on the *uncertainty* as to whether or not we *might* use such weapons. Even to encourage a potential aggressor to believe that we would be willing to use such weapons (even if we genuinely did not know ourselves whether or not we would) is still 'conjuring with the morally unthinkable', and an abandonment of a clear quest for international justice.

There is a fourth argument, however, which could allow for the retention of nuclear weapons without any intention to use them.

Psychological deterrent

We return now to Helmut Thielicke, who agrees that *if* the deterrent effect of nuclear weapons does imply a resolution to use them, then Christians are bound to unilateral renunciation of nuclear weapons. However, it is this implication which he questions.

He believes that it is a false approach to argue about deterrence in terms of intentions to use. If the goal of deterring aggression rests on a psychological consideration, then that consideration must be thought through *psychologically.* As he sees it, the deterrent effect of such weapons is not primarily related to an intention to use them. 'The point is not whether I am resolved to use nuclear weapons if needed, but whether my opponent *thinks* I am. These are two different things.'[11] The deterrent effect of my possession of nuclear weapons is only partly dependent on my convincing an enemy that I am resolved to use them. What matters more is to what extent he is himself similarly resolved. 'He, too, knows the destructive potential of nuclear weapons. If he rates it so highly that in the interest of self-preservation he regards their use as out of the question, then he will not lightly assume that I am resolved to use them either. He will instead believe that I am *un*prepared to use them in an emergency, but he will believe this only to the degree that he himself feels constrained to prevent any such emergency from arising.'[12] The psychological balance on which mutual deterrence depends, then, is the balance of 'equal unreadiness to use' on each side. The psychology of the situation, in Thielicke's mind, then has an inbuilt, stabilizing effect. I attribute to the enemy only such readiness or unreadiness to use weapons as I have myself. Each opponent judges the other's capabilities and intentions by his own. Whatever judgment he makes of his opponent is related to his own judgment of himself. *Either way* this leads to a balance.

Thielicke's argument thus suggests that deterrence can be maintained without any essential intention to use weapons, or any need for bluff. Possession of them is sufficient to deter, because the opponent is sufficiently uncertain.

A case could then be made (though Thielicke does not argue this) for the retention of a minimal deterrent force of strategic nuclear weapons, that they be held on station, but that all use of them be publicly forsworn. There would be no intention to use. There would be public rejection of any commitment to use. But their *presence* would create sufficient uncertainty in a potential aggressor's mind to deter him from aggressive action against us, and they could be used as a bargaining counter in negotiations.

In reply to Thielicke, it could be suggested that it is not necessarily clear that each side would judge their enemy by their own readiness or unreadiness, nor is it clear whether the build-up of other weapons systems (such as new conventional weapons, and lasers in space) would affect the psychological balance of nuclear weapons. Furthermore, to base a policy of deterrence on mere possession of nuclear weapons, without any intention to use, can only be effective on the assumption that the enemy would be sufficiently uncertain of my trustworthiness in order not to be sure of my declared intention not to use. In other words, the message that I am conveying to him is still that, if provoked, he cannot be sure that I would not act recklessly. It is not a message of the fundamental importance of the quest for justice in international relations.

On balance, therefore, despite the persuasiveness of Thielicke's brilliant psychological argument, it seems to me that mere possession of nuclear weapons of indiscriminate destructive power would need more solid moral argument in its favour in order to outweigh the force of the contrary moral view, namely that the only responsible course of action is to throw them away.

What is clear, as Thielicke himself acknowledges, is that 'the atomic peace which it [the psychological balance] establishes is more dangerous than any other peace based on fear. For in spite of the described balance and neutralising effect, it is conceivable that unexpected sparks will set fire to the powder, and that the necessary balance of atomic powers will then give place to a sudden world catastrophe. To envisage this possibility one has only to conjure up the apocalyptic vision of a Hitler having nuclear power at his disposal and dragging the whole world down with him. This is why atomic peace can never be a settled and reassuring peace. On the contrary, it will demand that we use all our powers to achieve an atomic disarmament on both sides.'[13]

It seems, then, that the Christian judgment has to be made between two possible alternatives. On the one hand we could decide to keep some nuclear weapons but forswear all possible use of them, relying on the uncertainty that such possession would create in the mind of a potential aggressor.

One would have to recognize that peace so achieved would be a very fragile peace indeed. On the other hand we could judge that weapons designed for indiscriminate mass destruction are themselves intrinsically immoral, and so reliance on them must be abandoned even though this would leave nuclear power on one side with no nuclear capability on the other, and would entail the risk of inviting aggression or blackmail.

The primary emphasis of the first way forward seems to be 'the risks of abandonment are too great', whereas that of the second seems to be 'despite all risks, the only morally responsible course is to abandon any reliance on nuclear weapons'. It is the latter view which I find the more persuasive – which makes the search for alternatives to nuclear deterrence very pressing indeed.

Notes for chapter fifteen

[1] R. Harries (ed.), *What Hope in an Armed World?* (Pickering and Inglis, 1982), p.99.

[2] Bishop Leonard in F. Bridger (ed.), *The Cross and the Bomb: Christian Ethics and the Nuclear Debate* (Mowbrays, 1983), p.7.

[3] H. Thielicke, *Theological Ethics*, **2** (English Translation, Eerdmans, 1969), p.479. [4] *Ibid.* [5] *Ibid.*

[6] M. Novak, *National Review*, 1 April 1983, p.382f.

[7] *Ibid.* [8] *Ibid.*

[9] R. Ruston, *Nuclear Deterrence – Right or Wrong?* (Catholic Information Services, 1981), p.62.

[10] O. M. T. O'Donovan, *Third Way*, **6** (10), November 1983.

[11] H. Thielicke, *op.cit.*, p.484. [12] *Ibid.* [13] *Ibid.*, p.486.

16 Alternatives

We seem to have reached the stage in our argument, therefore, which on the one hand has to acknowledge that in fact the West is placing very heavy weight indeed on the theory of nuclear deterrence, and on the other hand find that the moral basis of such dependence is too thin to support it. It is, however, one thing to say that nuclear deterrence is morally unacceptable. It is another to decide how politically we should respond to this judgment. It is not necessarily obvious that the right decision immediately to extricate ourselves from the immorality of deterrence is simply to opt for a unilateral decision to abandon the weapons we have. To quote Ruston again:

> In climbing down from an immoral practice, we must have a mind to the consequences of the way we do it; the timing, the effect it will have on the behaviour of others, *etc.* To think this way is not to advocate a situation ethics, it is simply to point out the obvious: that consequences – especially when they might take the form of a million deaths – are of vital importance in deciding the right way to act, even when the act in question is that of renouncing some immoral practice.[1]

This proper caution about method, however, is very far indeed from being the same thing as regarding nuclear deterrence as morally acceptable. Deterrentists believe that the possession of nuclear weapons for the purpose of deterrence is morally right. I agree with Ruston that such possession is morally wrong, must be renounced, and ways found to avoid this trap in which we have caught ourselves. Prudence, however, will dictate that any action is taken most cautiously.

I promised not to stray very far into specific political judgments, but it would be improper not to suggest courses of action which seem to me consistent with the moral judgments to which I have come. One particular course, advocated strongly by the Union of Concerned Scientists and supported by such eminent leaders as Field Marshal Lord Carver, Professor George Kennan, Robert McNamara and Lord Zuckerman, is that the West should move towards a No First Use Declaration as soon as broad agreement between Allied governments has been reached, and a proposed programme of conventional military improvements adequately advanced. After surveying the diplomatic and military considerations involved in making such a Declaration, the report *No First Use*[2] examines the existing balance of forces in Central Europe and elsewhere, and finds that it would be possible for Allied conventional forces to pose a serious counter to conventional attack without recourse to nuclear weapons. They believe, however, that Allied conventional forces need to be strengthened, and their report explores the cost of measures needed for such strengthening. They conclude that a No-First-Use Declaration by NATO would 'markedly reduce the danger of nuclear war and enhance the security of the US and its allies'. The processes leading to such a declaration should, they say, be set in motion forthwith. This policy is in marked and welcome contrast to present immoral NATO strategy which seems to be based on a possible first use or early use of nuclear weapons.

If abandonment of all nuclear weapons is the long-term objective – which I believe it must be – it would seem essential that this be coupled with a commitment to maintaining and developing alternative, non-nuclear defences. It is important at this point, however, to stress that within the requirements of the just war criteria, such defences would need to be, and to be seen to be, clearly defensive. This would call in question some of the recent NATO thinking on non-nuclear conventional weapons, and the desire of some strategists to make use of increasingly sophisticated 'conventional' weapons of immense destructive power ('a few kilotons') which are being developed by new technology.

One such proposal would be for the development of a conventional force of such weapons capable of responding to a Soviet conventional attack on Western Europe with a 'deep strike' attack on second and subsequent echelons of Soviet forces still deep in Warsaw Pact territory. Such 'deep strike' would seek to contain further Soviet advance by taking the action back over Warsaw Pact land. But it would need very long-range and highly accurate weapons, which military technologists are now making available. In order for such long-distance weapons to avoid the charge of indiscriminateness and hence immorality, their targetting would, how-ever, need to be very accurate indeed, and some com-mentators suggest that this is by no means clear. There seems in some minds a willingness to allow defence strategy to be shaped by available technology and promised technological advances, rather than to harness technology to moral goals. Furthermore, there is every likelihood that such proposed long-range conventional weapons would be perceived as aggressive and not as defensive weapons, and could well lead to a conventional arms race between the superpowers. The 4% increase in NATO defence spending which would be needed for the development of 'deep strike' conventional weapons could perhaps be better used for anti-tank and anti-aircraft weapons which can be seen to be purely defensive.

A non-nuclear defence for the West would involve serious change of priorities about the role of conventional forces. It would mean a willingness on the part of Western govern-ments to rethink the strategy on which Western defence is based. It would mean a willingness to face the costs involved and to relate Western defence costs to the wider needs for a more just distribution of the earth's resources. (How many lives are lost in the Third World *because* of allocation of our resources on an arms race?) It would also mean an acknow-ledgment of the serious risks of nuclear aggression or of nuclear blackmail. However, for a Christian committed to the view that what God requires of us is the preservation of life and of the order which is necessary for life to be lived, such risks may have to be taken. While on the one hand we are required to provide a restraint against evil aggression, our restraint itself must be seen to be just. We need a theology which helps us live with the risks which our quest for justice will entail. In the last analysis, this may involve a willingness to do what justice allows, and then to cast ourselves on the mercy of God.

Further political responses would have to be consistent with attempts to change direction in the priorities of the West from dependence on nuclear deterrence. Such a change might include a freeze on the production, deployment and testing of any further nuclear weapons. Such a freeze could be significant in the ever-twisting spiral of the 'steel triangle'.

The question as to the means by which abandonment of nuclear weapons could be achieved is primarily a matter for prudential political judgment. Provided the commitment to renounce such weapons is there, there could be a case for some 'prudential prevarication' for the time being, while conventional forces are strengthened and negotiating possibilities exploited. But that cannot go on indefinitely. It cannot go on for long. Strategic nuclear weapons (and in my view battlefield weapons also) must eventually be abandoned.

The political judgment about means has to weigh several considerations. On the one hand, in moral terms, the utterly indiscriminate strategic weapons are the most abhorrent. On the other hand, they are perhaps less likely to be used than the increasingly accurate counterforce battlefield (theatre) weapons, which have blurred the distinction between nuclear and conventional weapons and made it more 'thinkable' actually to use tactical weapons in Europe. David Owen makes this judgment in *Face the Future*[3]: 'There would be great security advantages in negotiating away all of NATO's and the Warsaw Pact's short range battlefield weapons and putting this as a higher priority than some of the strategic arms limitation issues, important though they are.' To have as a shorter term goal the negotiation of a nuclear-free zone in central Europe could be one step away from the likelihood of first strike use of tactical weapons which could lead to a strategic exchange. On the other hand, is this prudence at the cost of morality? Should not the 'intrinsically' immoral strategic weapons be disposed of first? Would the international scene be more stable (as well as less immoral) without the strategic weapons, while the battlefield weapons are kept until conventional forces are up to strength? Much of this involves prudential political judgment. The questions are thorny ones, now that we have based so much reliance on nuclear weapons for so long. Unilateral, wholesale, immediate nuclear disarmament might be very destabilizing. But there is no doubt about the direction we should face: reduction and urgent progress towards abandonment rather than escalation is imperative. And both sides have *enormous* margins within which to take unilateral steps.

Alongside such military and political possibilities, there is a range of diplomatic, cultural, educational and religious initiatives which could be explored to build trust, gain knowledge of the 'other side' and construct institutions based on justice which can further peace. The sad fact is that the supreme sense of emergency fostered by reliance on nuclear deterrence blurs our vision of other, more spiritual, realities, forces us away from trust into deeper mistrust, makes words like 'reconciliation' or even 'co-existence' harder to hear, and hampers the search for more just relationships between nations. We do well to recall President Kennedy's speech made at the American University as far back as June 1963. He spoke about peace thus:

> ... not a Pax Americana enforced in the world by American weapons of war. ... I am talking about genuine peace, the kind of peace that makes life on earth worth living, the kind that enables men and nations to grow and to hope and to build a better life for their children – not merely peace for Americans, but peace for all men and women. ... Some say that it is useless to speak of peace or world law or world disarmament – and that it will be useless until the leaders of the Soviet Union adopt a more enlightened attitude. I hope they do. I believe we can help them to do it. But I also believe that we must re-examine our own attitude – as individuals and as a Nation – for our attitude is as essential as theirs. ... No government or social system is so evil that its people must be considered as lacking in virtue. As Americans we find communism profoundly repugnant as a negation of personal freedom and dignity. But we can still hail the Russian people for their many achievements – in science and space, in economic and

industrial growth, in culture and in acts of courage. . . . So let us not be blind to our differences – but let us also direct attention to our common interests and the means by which those differences can be resolved. And if we cannot end now our differences, at least we can help make the world safe for diversity. For, in the final analysis, our most basic common link is that we all inhabit this small planet. We all breathe the same air. We all cherish our children's future. And we are all mortal.[4]

While trust is placed primarily in 'chariots and horses' instead of in the living God in whose world we are called to work for justice and for peace, our moral sense becomes dimmed, our priorities go awry, our vision is blurred. It is where there is no vision of God and his ways, as the wise man said so long ago, the people perish.

Notes for chapter sixteen

[1] R. Ruston, *Nuclear Deterrence – Right or Wrong?* (Catholic Information Service, 1981), p.63.
[2] Union of Concerned Scientists, 1983.
[3] D. Owen, *Face the Future* (OUP, 1981), p.228.
[4] President John F. Kennedy, quoted in G. Prins (ed.), *Defended to Death* (Penguin, 1983), p.123.

Part 5

What hope for James?

Dear James,

You asked for some help in making up your mind as a Christian student about war. I am not sure whether this is quite what you bargained for!

I hope that you have seen how important it is to try to think *theologically*, but how difficult and complex moral decisions can be! I think you may be a little disappointed that I do not draw more specifically from the biblical text to settle the issues decisively. I wish it were that easy. It seems to me that the Bible is given to us not as a moral textbook, but as a guide for knowing God. We need to think about ourselves and our world from a perspective drawn from the biblical witness to Christ, but I think we mistake the purpose for which God gave us the Bible if we think that it will give us ready answers to contemporary political questions.

I believe, however, that a biblical theological analysis of our human predicament and of the moral task for Christians in this area gives us a firm basis on which to struggle with these complex issues, and also promises us the resources of God's grace to hold on to in our uncertainties. God's Word makes sense of our apparently senseless world, and holds out to us the promise of his grace. There *can* be a peace in our time, a peace in our experience, a peace in our relationships, but this is not a peace which belongs to this world order, and cannot be attained by treaty or conference. The peace of God which passes all understanding, and which keeps our hearts and minds, is a peace 'in Christ Jesus'. In him alone can a deep peace be found. When Cranmer borrowed a phrase from the 1545 Prymer of Henry VIII and wrote it into the Church of England services for Morning and Evening Prayer, it was this peace I think he had in mind: 'Give peace in our time, O Lord; because there is none other that fighteth for us, but only Thou, O God.'

That God is 'for us' is also the message of the rainbow. We recall the covenant made with Noah, the word of God's grace towards his fallen world after the flood. The rainbow stands as his promise that even this fallen world is held within his care. This world order cannot perish by its own destructive wickedness while God holds his world in being. And while the earth remains, his providential ordering is promised. That should be a word of comfort to us in the face of the fatalism and despair of some of our contemporaries. Despite all the uncertainty and all the horror which modern technological warfare can evoke, 'he has the whole wide world in his hands' and the peace of Christ can rule in our hearts.

That is not to say, of course, that there is not a measure of peace worth working for between societies and peoples within this world order. On the contrary, our Christian calling to be peacemakers does not stop at the proclamation of the gospel of peace with God through faith in Christ. It commits us also to making peace where and when we can. But we need to remember that the peace achieved through treaty, through negotiation, through conventions of restraint in the uses of power, is very far from the peace of Christ. It can only ever be an anxious peace, a fragile peace, a peace based on balances of power. The peace we can and must seek to achieve through political means – a conventional peace – is not Christ's peace. But we who know Christ's peace can be set free from the fear and the anxiety which sometimes paralyses any search even for this limited conventional peace.

The peace from above drives us to seek peace on earth all the more.

I hope that our journey through some biblical themes has shown you how important it is, however, to approach the political questions of peace-making first of all by way of the questions of order and justice. We need a theology of order before we can know what it means to work for peace. At this point our discussion of the state is so crucial. I am not sure whether you will share my theology of the state, but it is only when you have made up your mind about that, that it will become at all clear to you how to approach the questions of war.

You may come to believe that in conscience you must be a pacifist. I have a great deal of sympathy with you. I cannot, however, follow you all the way. To do so seems to me to lead to a position in which I would be obliged to require others to make sacrifices which can properly only be decided within each individual conscience, and which would lead to an abandonment of justice and an aquiescence in unrestrained evil.

You may, like me, believe that force must sometimes be used by the state in the cause of justice. I hope you will agree, though, that the Christian can have no place for a crusading militarism in his thinking, and we must do all we can to rid our society of such attitudes. It is surely indisputable that much modern weaponry being indiscriminate by design and total in effect has changed the moral scene in recent years. I hope you will agree with me that any use of such weapons would be utterly immoral, and must not happen. I wonder whether you will share my view that the theory of nuclear deterrence is morally unacceptable, and together with its inherent instability is a most unsatisfactory basis on which to place so much reliance. This at least is the point I have come to in my thinking so far. I sometimes wonder whether I have taken what Thielicke calls 'the ethical borderline' seriously enough, and whether under the rubric of divine mercy and forgiveness we may not be required to get our hands dirtier than I believe is morally permissible. Specifically, is there a sufficient moral case still to be made for the mere possession of nuclear weapons (while forswearing all use) to create sufficient uncertainty in a potential aggressor's mind that he would be deterred from using his weapons? I am myself not convinced. But if my argument is right, then the pressing question is how as a nation – as a world – we can extricate ourselves from our reliance on these horrific weapons. We have glanced at some of the political options.

Whichever view you come to, I urge you to contribute in whatever way you can towards the growth of structures for peace, and the maintenance of conventions in the restraints of power. You recall my quotation from President Kennedy? The world has changed since 1963, but our common humanity under God has not. Let us pursue all that makes for peace and builds up our common life.

In the pursuit of such peace we must work for justice. We must not lose sight of the righteousness of God who makes justice possible, nor of our responsibilities for working for justice within this fallen world. As we have said before, we owe it to God and to our fellow men to see to it that our social institutions serve the cause of justice and of peace. It is in that perspective that I hope you can see your role as a citizen under God. We need here, however, to sound a note of caution. As Christians we need to be particularly aware that it is one thing to talk about moral issues. It is another thing to have available the detailed information on which political and military decisions have to be made. It is yet a third thing to have responsibility for making them. There has to be a recognition of the difficulty of holding together the absolute questions of moral principle and the compromise questions of political judgment.

Furthermore, as we have said, the changing political scene changes the ethical questions which are being asked. It would have been a different question to ask about the morality of making nuclear weapons when no other nation had done so – different from the question *we* face about the morality of keeping nuclear weapons now that other nations do have them. The theological and ethical task is not finished. It needs to be constantly undertaken afresh. But the confidence we have to engage in it, and the obligation to do so, derive from the peace of the gospel which we are also committed to proclaim. What issue more clearly than this should drive us on in our task of engaging theologically with our world, and in a deep and contemporary preaching of Christ's gospel?

There are, of course, many important relevant themes which we have not had time to look at. We have not opened up the question of whether there can be a just revolution; we have only touched briefly on liberation theology; we have not explored the problems of conscription or of conscientious objection; we have not probed at all into some of the ethical borderline issues of the conduct of war – the ethical dilemmas of intelligence gathering, of the conflicts of truth and life, of deceit, of coercive force in the treatment of prisoners who may hold information essential for the safety of others; we have not unpacked any of the situational dilemmas in weighing the loss of some lives for the sake of saving many more. What I hope we have done is begin to explore a way of setting up a theological, ethical approach to some of these questions, and providing a framework in which they can be worked on.

But to many of these and other questions there is not a straightforward 'Christian answer'. And that applies in some of the personal decisions you face also. I cannot tell you whether you should join the army, or should work for 'defence' with your engineering degree. I cannot tell you whether you should join a peace movement, protest against Cruise, or march at political rallies. I can tell you that there will be wars and rumours of wars, even though we must do all that we can to avert them. In the world, our Lord said, there will be tribulation. But be of good cheer, he has overcome the world. Some of his apostles could look forward only to persecution, and who knows whether that may be asked of any of us. But Christ has suffered for us, leaving us an example that we should follow in his steps.

Our reading of the present world scene may drive us back to Jeremiah's words, with his warnings about the hand of divine judgment against nations which have abandoned God. Part of our Christian task is to express to our nation her responsibilities before God. With so much reliance being placed on immoral and unjust postures of retaliation as the basis for national security, are we not as a nation becoming weighed down with the guilt of having abandoned the cause of justice? A politics which knows anything of forgiveness can be willing to make the first moves towards conciliation, and would refuse only to match threat with destructive counter-threat. The Christian citizen can call the politician to a politics based on a moral understanding of what justice touched with forgiveness might require. The Christian citizen must face the politician with these critical and painful questions of conscience and remind him of his heavy responsibilities for government under God. Is Jeremiah's word not a word for today?

I do urge you, through all this, to bring your personal and political judgments into the light of the fact that this is God's world and you are called to live as one of his covenant people. When you are tempted to be despondent and despairing, wondering whether the kingdom of Christ will ever be seen, that is the time (as Isaiah of old encouraged the people of his day) to turn back to a meditation on the majesty of God (Is.40:12f.). May that give you confidence to interpret our world theologically to our contemporaries, and may it give you opportunity for a confident preaching of the gospel of peace in Christ.

For it is God's purpose in the fulness of time to unite all things in Christ, things in heaven and things on earth. This conviction will deliver you from the fatalism of your friends, who see nothing but despair ahead of them. It will help you remember that Christ comes to his world, and that despite all that may happen to this world order, we wait for new heavens and a new earth in which righteousness dwells. We look for the day when death shall be no more, neither shall there be mourning nor crying nor pain any more. We look for the day when the river of the water of life will flow from the throne of God and of the Lamb. And either side of the river, there is the tree of life. The leaves of the tree, the prophet assures us, are for the healing of the nations.

Direct this and every nation in the ways of justice and of peace: that men may honour one another, and seek the common good.

Lord, in your mercy, hear our prayer.

Suggestions for further reading

Bainton, R. H., *Christian Attitudes to War and Peace*. Hodder, 1961.

Bridger, F. (ed.), *The Cross and the Bomb: Christian Ethics and Nuclear Debate*. Mowbrays, 1983.

Church of England Board for Social Responsibility, *The Church and the Bomb*. Hodder, 1983.

Ellul, J., *Violence*. Mowbrays, 1978.

Harries, R. (ed.), *What Hope in an Armed World?* Pickering and Inglis, 1982.

Holmes, A., *War and Christian Ethics*. Baker, 1978. (Historical reading.)

Hornus, J. N., *It is Not Lawful for Me to Fight*: Early Christian Attitudes Towards War, Violence and the State. Paternoster, 1980.

Miller Jr., W., *A Canticle for Leibowitz*. Corgi, 1959. (A novel.)

Paskins, B. and Dockrill, M., *The Ethics of War*. Duckworth, 1981.

Prins, G. (ed.), *Defended to Death*. Penguin, 1983.

Ramsey, P., *War and the Christian Conscience*. Duke University Press, 1961.

Ruston, R., *Nuclear Deterrence – Right or Wrong?* Catholic Information Services, 1981.

Sider, R. and Taylor, R., *Nuclear Holocaust and Christian Hope*. Hodder, 1982.

Thielicke, H., *Theological Ethics*, **2**. English Translation, Eerdmans, 1969.

Towle, P., Elliot, I. and Frost, G., *Protest and Perish – a Critique of Unilateralism*. Institute for European Defence and Strategic Studies, 1982.

Walzer, M., *Just and Unjust Wars*. Penguin, 1980.

Williams, R., *The Truce of God*. Fount, 1983.